# HOW TO BUILD
# YOUR OWN BOAT
# FROM SCRATCH

## BY JOHN TRAISTER

# TAB BOOKS
### BLUE RIDGE SUMMIT, PA. 17214

FIRST EDITION

FIRST PRINTING—MAY 1978

Copyright © 1978 by TAB BOOKS

Printed in the United States
of America

**Library of Congress Cataloging in Publication Data**

Traister, John E.
    How to build your own boat from scratch.

    Includes index.
    1. Boat-building—Amateurs' manuals. I. Title.
VM321.T7        623.82'02        77-18927
ISBN 0-8306-8923-0
ISBN 0-8306-7923-5 pbk.

Cover photo courtesy of Luger Industries, Inc.

# HOW TO BUILD YOUR OWN BOAT FROM SCRATCH

**Other TAB books by the author:**

# Preface

The romance between man and boat goes back into ancient history and continues to this day. In fact, boating is what the industry calls America's "top family sport." And no wonder, figures of the National Association of Marine Engine and Boat Manufacturers say that nearly 50 million people in this country own 10 million boats and have spent more than $4 million in the process of buying and maintaining them! Yes, boating is truly a family sport, and owning your own boat today is as normal as owning a second car.

The ideal of building your own boat has a mystique all its own, and once you know how easy building your own can be, nothing remains but to choose the type of boat you want and build it. The finished product will be unique because your energy shaped each curve and turned each screw. Later, when you're sailing your craft alone or with companions, your satisfaction will sharpen because you'll know every inch of the boat you've built and you'll understand exactly what it will do.

While it is true that many types of boats should only be attempted by master craftsmen—those with several projects under their belts—the boats described in this book are for people like you, the amateur boatbuilder. If you can handle basic hand tools, you will have no problems with the designs discussed here. If you're somewhat in doubt concerning the use of some of the tools, then Chapter 2 will guide you in the right direction. Chapter 3 will then tell you how to select and buy the proper materials...from whom and from where.

Several designs are given—for fishing boats, pirogues, kayaks, canoes, and sailboats. If you don't see what you want, we have even included the sources for obtaining other plans of practically any design that comes to mind. If you aren't sure exactly what you want, then Chapter 1 will help you decide.

Maybe you already have a fine boat that meets your needs. Then refer to the chapters on boat repairs and maintenance for keeping your pride and joy in tip-top condition.

This book could not have been written without the help of the many manufacturers and retailers of boat plans, kits, supplies, and materials. I have tried to include all of their names in the book under the chapter(s) where their material was used. I am especially indebted to naval architect Glen L. Witt of Bellflower, Calif., for permission to use illustrations of his many boat designs.

John Traister

# Contents

# What Type Of Boat Do You Want?

Except for those who depend upon a certain type of boat to make their living, the main reason for a new boat is normally for pleasure. The acquisition of a pleasure boat can be compared to the purchase of a second car or perhaps a second home—like a vacation cabin on the beach, in the mountains, or by a lake or stream. Since a boat—unlike a family car or a full-time residence—is not absolutely necessary, we can take longer to decide upon the type that would most closely fit our needs, budget, and the like. Then when we do shell out those hard-earned dollars for a kit or materials to build the craft, we can rest assured that the type of craft selected comes as close as possible to fulfilling our desires and needs as our budget will allow.

Still, many people either don't take the time or don't know how to choose a boat that will enable them to make every dollar count. This fate, however, can be avoided by a little study. Then with nearly two dozen types of craft and any number of variations and mutations to choose from, there's really no reason for not having the boat that is best suited to your individual needs. What then are the basic steps in finding the right boat for you and your family?

First and most important is to decide upon the *one* activity in which you will use your boat the most. Will it be used mostly for fishing trips in inland rivers or streams…mostly in bays and coastal waters for cruising or water skiing…or on some of the larger lakes where you and your family spend the weekends? Perhaps the boat will be used only for hunting ducks in the marshes around your home. There are many decisions, but once settled, begin thinking about the other activities—in order of their importance—which the boat may be called upon to participate in. Then decide upon the number of people you expect the boat to carry, the type of waters in which it will be used the most, and how the boat will be transported. When all of these decisions have been made, you will have a sound basis for selecting a boat that will come pretty close to answering all of your boating needs.

To further illustrate the selection of a boat, let's assume that most of your boating activities will consist of float fishing on some of the smaller inland rivers—those with varying water depths, a few rapids, and calm water in general. At this point, any number of boat types would be suited to the situation: a john boat, a rowboat, pirogue, canoe, or kayak. But let's look a bit further before jumping to a hasty conclusion. Past experience tells us that most days on the river will find you alone because your work prevents you from making plans for fishing with others; you have to sieze the moment, then load your boat and fishing gear and take off for the nearest river. Still, you want to have a boat that will carry more than one person for those days you and your buddies can get together. From this we also know that the boat will have to be light enough for loading and unloading by one person. Of course, with the proper boat trailer, even a very large boat can be launched by a single person—provided a proper landing is available. Again your past experience on these rivers convinces you that landings are not readily available and you remember several times when you had to carry or drag your boat several feet from the road to the river bank. Therefore, the type of craft chosen will have to be suitable for one or two people and weigh less than 100 pounds.

Let's further assume that your secondary activities will include an occasional float trip down these same rivers during the winter months as you flush ducks from the many bends. You may also want to use the boat to check your muskrat traps along the rivers and tributaries. With all of these facts, most of us would probably agree that a light canoe or kayak would be ideal. However, a little more investigation might prove that another craft would be suited best to your activities.

On their first boat project, many people overlook dozens of things that should have been considered before beginning the project. For example, one person didn't take into consideration the varying depths of the waters around his home before purchasing a boat. Now he has a $3500 boat, but spends more time wading and pushing it off sand bars than he does riding in it! Another man invested a couple of hundred dollars in a metal boat to use near his home in Beaufort, S.C. In a few short months the craft looked like a fishing seine due to the corrosive effect of the salt water. The cases are endless.

Many of these mistakes can be avoided if you acquire a basic knowledge of boats in general, then find out the advantages and disadvantages of each type. Begin by reading through as many nautical journals as you can get your hands on; attend boat shows and listen to what the manufacturers' representatives have to say; talk to some of the "Old Salts" down at the small-boat basin; observe other boats in operation. All of these things can help you make the right decision when it comes to selecting your own boat.

To further assist you in your selection, the paragraphs to follow are designed to take you on a brief cruise through the more general types of boats which are best suited to amateur boatbuilding. Since these are general types, you'll find that many boats tend to bridge the type divisions. However, if you look a little closer, you'll see that any particular boat will have attributes that qualify it as one of the types mentioned in this chapter. The modifications have been done for a specific purpose—for tailoring the boat to a certain type of use, for power purposes, or perhaps only for satisfying the desires of the owner.

## FUN BOATS

Practically any boat can be classified as a "fun boat," but there are certain types that have no other purpose than use for fun. There are dozens of boat designs that can be described as "fun boats." If you and your family are beach addicts or "swimsuit" sailers, then a paddleboard or sailboard will certainly not go unused on your outings. Just about anybody can build his own paddleboard, even the

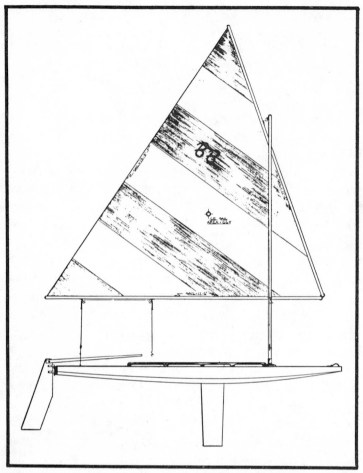

Fig. 1-1. If you and your family are beach addicts or "swimsuit" sailors, then a sailboat like this one would be ideal.

kids, with a little help from you. In fact, many boat kits are available which provide the necessary plans, framing members, and all the fastenings in one simple and inexpensive package. All you do is add a sheet or two of standard sized plywood, a few lengths of lumber, some glue, and a little spare time for some real fun and pleasure for the whole family.

Paddleboards come in standard sizes from 8 feet to 12 feet. The 8-foot lengths are perfect for a single adult or a couple of kids, while the longer models are good load carriers—capable of handling a couple of adults or several kids. If built perfectly watertight, these models are impossible to sink and their light weight makes them easy to carry. You can load one or several into the station wagon, pickup, or even transport it on the roof of the family car. These models can be used on just about any protected body of water, such as a lake, stream, or bay; they can even be used as surfboards at the beaches.

Sailboards, like the one shown in Fig. 1-1, are similar to paddleboards, except that the sailboard is equipped with a sail, rudder, and centerboard for stability. The rigging, however, is simple enough to knock down so that the entire package will fit in a station wagon or on top of the car. These little sailers can provide a lot of thrills and, when filled with flotation, make excellent sailing trainers.

If you're one who likes his boating a little drier, there's a wide variety of pontoon deck boats that strongly resemble floating patios. They provide excellent porch space for sunbathing, swimming or fishing parties, or just plain talking with guests. There's also plenty of room for the charcoal broiler so you can have barbecues and fish fries aboard your floating patio. When camouflaged, the sturdy deck makes an excellent platform for waterfowl shooting. In fact, I'll bet you have already thought of a dozen other uses for a floating deck like this.

Just about anyone can build his own pontoon boat, even if his woodworking experience has been limited to splitting firewood for his barbecue pit. Once the basic platform is completed, you are free to choose from an endless number of possibilities for the top. Perhaps you'll use it for a swimming raft like the one in Fig. 1-2. With an awning and guardrail attached (Fig. 1-3), it is perfect for family fishing, picnicking, or leisurely day-cruising with an outboard motor

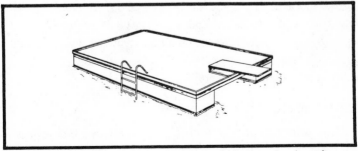

Fig. 1-2. A floating platform is frequently used as a swimming raft.

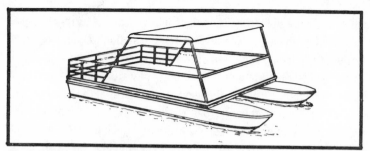

Fig. 1-3. When an awning and guardrail are attached to a floating platform, it is perfect for family fishing, picnicking, or day-cruising.

for power. A cabin added to the platform makes it suitable for camping and extended cruises on lakes and other protected waters; such a conversion can be seen in Fig. 1-4.

## DINGHIES

The dinghy was originally used as a means of getting to and from the mooring of a large yacht, but in recent years, when equipped with a sail, centerboard, and rudder, it has proven to be a very handy sailer. In fact, it is not unusual to see the owners of luxury yachts neglect their "pride and joy" in favor of the fun to be had with the yacht's dinghies.

The amateur boatbuilder will also find that a well-built dinghy will quickly capture his heart—either for sailing, rowing, or power-boating. Such a craft is both easy and inexpensive to build, has a multitude of practical uses, and is easily transported on top of the family car. You can take turns sailing your dinghy on lakes, bays, and other protected waters. When equipped with a small outboard motor, it provides excellent transportation around and across the boat basin, from one side of the lake (where your summer cottage is located) to the other (to see a neighbor); and there are dozens of other uses. It also makes a good base for skin diving activities and can easily and comfortably be used for any type of fishing on inland waters. Because of its many uses, the little 8- to 12-foot dinghy is hard to beat as a first boat project.

## HUNTING AND FISHING BOATS

The outdoorsman who waits in silence for that first flight of waterfowl on a cold winter morning, or the freshwater fisherman who combs the many shorelines and drops for that lunker bass, will be interested in stable, utilitarian crafts. This group of crafts includes the classic canoe, the kayak, and hunting punts. John boats, bass boats, and similar types are also included. But let's see exactly which type would best suit your hunting and fishing needs.

The punt of duck hunting type of boat is usually made in 12- and 14-foot lengths and is light and compact enough for one man to load atop his car. Still, it is roomy enough for two adults and all their gear. It ranges in weight between 80 and 125 pounds and will easily accept outboard motors from 5 to 7 1/2 HP.

The hunting punts float low in the water and are usually painted a dead grass color for use in waterfowl marshes. The design is excellent for fishing and other uses in protected waters. Many of these boats are fitted with three steel-stripped runners on the bottom of the hull so the craft can be dragged across snow and ice like a sled. For added stability in shallow water, these boats are fitted with four screw eyes to the outside clamps (two on each side); then 4 3/8″ × 40″ (or larger) steel rods are inserted through the eyes and driven into the shallow river bottom. These same screw eyes could also be used to lash the boat to an automobile carrier.

A flat bottom, double ended craft used by the natives of Louisiana, and called a pirogue, is another useful craft for hunting or fishing in shallow water. The typical pirogue is about 14 feet long, is lightweight, and can be built inexpensively from practically any type of wood. The Cajuns of the Louisiana Bayou country use this boat in

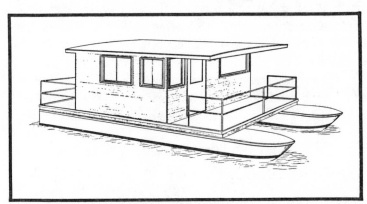

Fig. 1-4. A cabin added to the platform makes it suitable for camping and extended cruises.

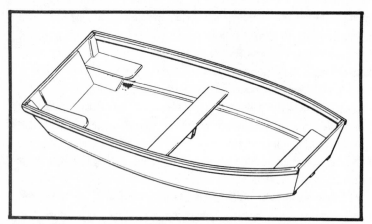

Fig. 1-5. A flat bottom john boat is another type of popular boat for hunting and fishing along streams and lakesides.

their daily routines of fishing, hunting, moss gathering, trapping, and transportation. The design has proved satisfactory over many decades. If you would like to build your own pirogue, refer to Chapter 8.

The flat bottom john boat in Fig. 1-5 is another type of popular boat for hunting and fishing along streams, bayous, and lakes. You can power such a boat with a small outboard motor, or you can row it, pole it, or scull it as you choose. Many of the older designs were made from 1-inch yellow pine board and were heavy as hell, but were able to take the bumps and bruises of practically any use you'd care to put it. Often a 3- or 4-foot length of 1″ × 8″ board was nailed upright in one end of these boats as shown in Fig. 1-6. Then when the sucker fish began their spring run around the first of March, the owners of these boats would use dip nets on long cedar poles to capture them; the board was used as a lever to lift the loaded nets.

The cost of building a john boat is always very low, and maintenance requires only a painting every year or two. It's an excellent type of boat for the beginner to undertake—especially if it's his first project.

Next in line would be the flat bottom row boats. They aren't fancy or streamlined, but they are still one of the most functional of all boats for hunting and fishing—not to mention for a family outing on the lake. The simply constructed flat bottom types of rowboats can do anything that the bigger, fancier jobs can do and will even outlast most of them. You can draw them up on a beach and walk ashore, something that isn't so easy with a vee bottom hull.

The flat bottom offers more stability than conventional hulls, and is ideal for cast fishing or for absorbing the recoil of a duck hunter's 12-gauge shotgun. As for riding ability, it will bring you back on any type of water a boat of this size and power should be out on. Most flat bottoms will accept outboard motors in the 3 to 5 HP range—plenty of power for normal uses.

The traditional canoe is ideal for car-top carrying, fly fishing, and exploring the shallow shorelines for game in a quiet manner. Most canoes are very lightweight for their respective lengths and can be handled, even carried, by one man. Their only drawbacks are that they're easily damaged and they will tip over easier than most other types of crafts. Building a canoe from scratch is normally a little too difficult for the beginner, but there are many kits on the market which offer this opportunity to anyone who can handle basic hand tools.

Many people believe that the kayak—both the original Eskimo version and many of its modified forms—is still the best all-around

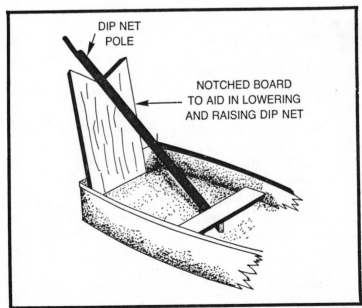

Fig. 1-6. Often a board is nailed upright in a flat bottom boat to act as a lever for raising and lowering dip nets.

one-man boat for hunting and fishing. When equipped with water-tight bulkheads, they can be used along coastal waters as well as on protected inland waters. Most designs provide weather-protected room for gear under the aft and fore decks. The average kayak is considered more stable than the canoe; moreover, they are as light and as easy to transport. Some varieties even come in a take-down or folding design.

The traditional way to propel a kayak is with a double-ended paddle, but with a special side bracket, it can be powered with a small outboard motor. Many kayaks have even been rigged for sailing. Chapter 6 gives complete instructions for building a modified kayak, a practical boat easily constructed by an amateur.

## CABIN CRUISERS

Cabin cruisers are normally selected by the owner only after careful consideration has been given to the size of his family or the number of people he will normally have aboard; he also considers the intended distances and activities of his cruises. All cabin cruisers have facilities for cooking, bunks and mattresses for sleeping under a solid roof, and an ample cockpit for chatter, eating, and card playing. Many cruisers have enough horses for ski-towing or a little on-plane cruising. The cost of any type of cabin cruiser is going to take a big hunk out of your bank account, but for the added pleasure derived by you and your family, the money will be well spent.

A small 17-foot cabin cruiser like the one in Fig. 1-7 is probably as large as the amateur boatbuilder would want to undertake. Still, this craft has a lot to offer the entire family for overnight cruising. It has a head, berths, and cooking facilities. The extra large cockpit provides sleeping bag space for additional sack-time artists. A convenient cabinet in the cabin converts into a semi-enclosed toilet room; opposite to the cabinet is a galley with sink and stove space. The bulkhead has a passthrough opening that provides service to the galley area. Obviously, this particular craft has all the features of an outboard cruiser, and yet is an ideal length for easy trailering behind the family car.

The craft shown in Fig. 1-8 is a complete family cruiser. When the dinette folds down, there are berths for three more people on the same level as the forward berths. The 12-foot long area provides

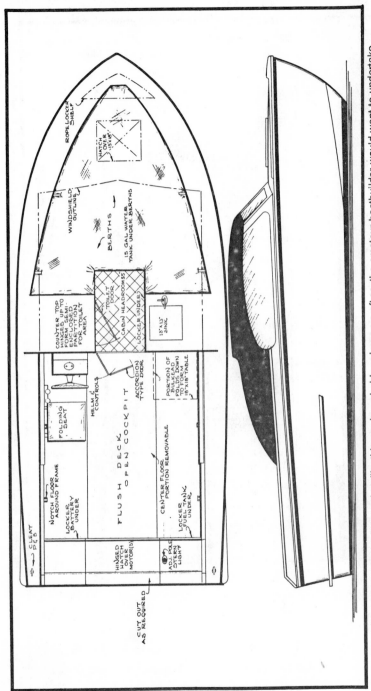

Fig. 1-7. A small 17-foot cabin cruiser like this one is probably as large a craft as the amateur boatbuilder would want to undertake.

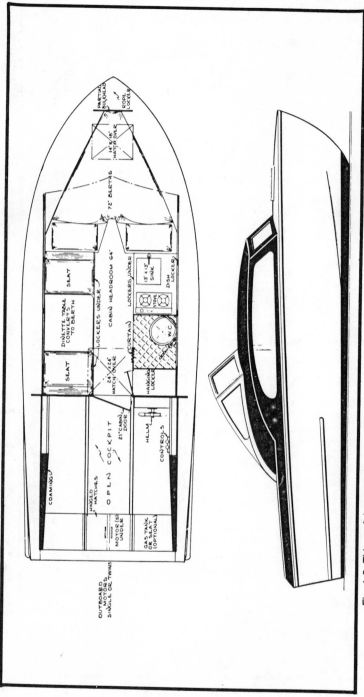

Fig. 1-8. This craft is a complete family cruiser with berths for three when the dinette is folded down.

plenty of sleeping space for extra tall crew members. The galley has enough room for all the necessary gear, including a sink, stove, refrigerator, etc. An enclosed head ensures privacy for everyone, and there's a hanging locker adjacent to the cabin entry. The large cockpit offers lots of space to enjoy diving, fishing, or mere lounging.

## CRUISING HOUSEBOATS

If you want to enjoy all the comforts of home and still want fast action on the water, then a cruising houseboat like the one shown in Fig. 1-9 is for you. This particular craft is really two boats in one: above the gunwale she's all houseboat, but below the rail she's all speedboat. Although perhaps not evident in the drawing, this houseboat has a modern vee bottom hull capable of speeds approaching 30 MPH.

The favorable features of houseboats include lots of room for sun bathing and deck fishing. Inside the cabin you'll find full headroom, provisions for sleeping four or more adults, and an enclosed toilet room. The galley will have sufficient space for the latest marine galley equipment, plus storage for cooking gear. Houseboats less than 25-feet long are usually trailerable, so take this into consideration if you're planning an excursion.

After studying the floor plan in Fig. 1-9, I'm certain that you'll agree with most people in saying that a houseboat provides a complete vacation cottage on the water.

## UTILITIES

If your desire is for higher performance with fewer frills, consider the large variety of utility boats. This type of boat probably comes the closest to being an all-purpose boat for bays and coastal waters. It is typified by a large open cockpit (see Fig. 1-10). It is the first choice of the boater who uses his craft for fishing, skin diving, camping, and towing skiers. It is highly adaptable and the boater will find that he can readily rig the craft to suit his own needs.

Despite the open cockpit, many utility boats have a raised deck line which gives a high freeboard forward and space for berths below deck. The raised deck line and wide beam keep these boats very dry when underway. Because this type of boat can accommodate a big engine, high speeds are possible. Yet the compact size makes it easy

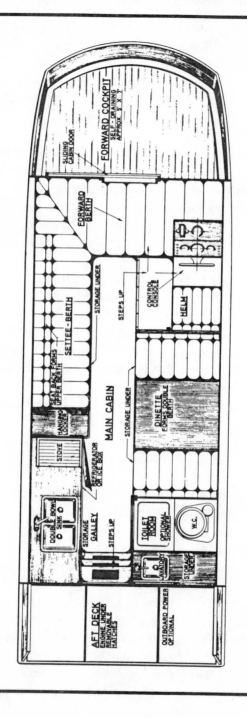

FORWARD COCKPIT
SELF - DRAINING
APPROX. 5' X 7'

SLIDING
CABIN DOOR

FORWARD
BERTH

SEAT BACK FORMS
UPPER BERTH

SETTEE - BERTH

STORAGE UNDER

STEPS UP

CONTROL
CONSOLE

HELM

HANGING
LOCKER

MAIN CABIN

STORAGE UNDER

DINETTE
FORMS DOUBLE
BERTH

STOVE

REFRIGERATOR
OR ICE BOX

DOUBLE BOWL
SINK

STORAGE
GALLEY

STEPS UP

TOILET
ROOM
OPTIONAL
SHOWER

W.C.

LAVATORY

STORAGE
UNDER

AFT DECK
ENGINE UNDER
REMOVABLE
HATCHES

OUTBOARD POWER
OPTIONAL

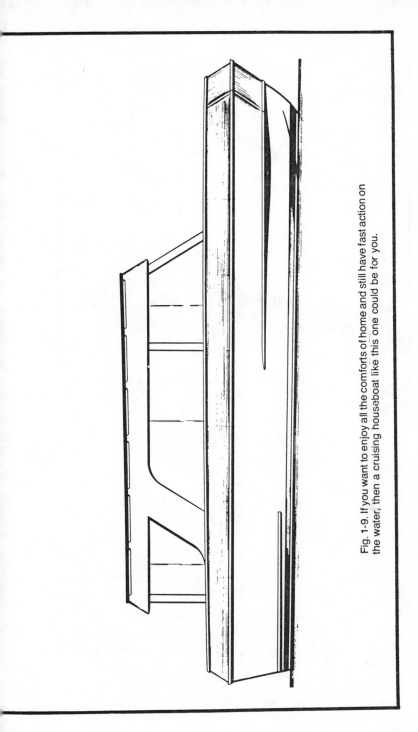

Fig. 1-9. If you want to enjoy all the comforts of home and still have fast action on the water, then a cruising houseboat like this one could be for you.

25

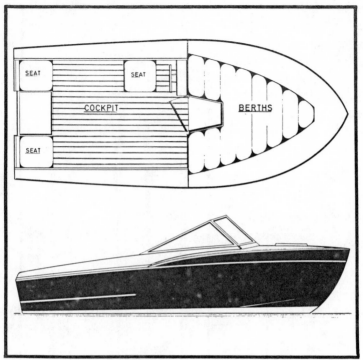

Fig. 1-10. An open cockpit typifies the utility boats. They're near to being an all-purpose type.

to trailer and launch. Such boats can be used for overnight camping and cruising, sport fishing, water skiing, or just about any water sport activity.

This type of boat may seem a little too complex for the average beginner, but frame kits are available for less than $200 which eliminate much of the more difficult cutting and fitting involved.

## SAILBOATS

There are many medium-sized, easily transported, sailing cruisers designed for single-handed sailing. Take the 17-foot overnight sloop in Fig. 1-11, for example. Sleeping facilities are provided for two, with space remaining for a folding toilet. Even with a portable ice box and stove, the cockpit has room for an auxiliary outboard motor and sail bin.

You can go, of course, to the larger sailing cruisers like the 30-foot cruising auxiliary in Fig. 1-12—if your pocketbook can afford it! A boat of this type is ideal for family vacation sailing where safety, comfort, minimum cost, and ease of handling are important. This craft has the characteristics for good cruising performance and is not designed to meet the capricious rules of racing.

The self-bailing aft cockpit can be used for sleeping in fair weather, and all sheets lead to the cockpit. There are no cramped vee-berths as with typical stock boats of this kind. The galley and head with shower are located amidships where space is greatest and motion is least. The four lower berths are oversize, and the backs of

Fig. 1-11. An easily transported sailing cruiser designed for single-handed sailing.

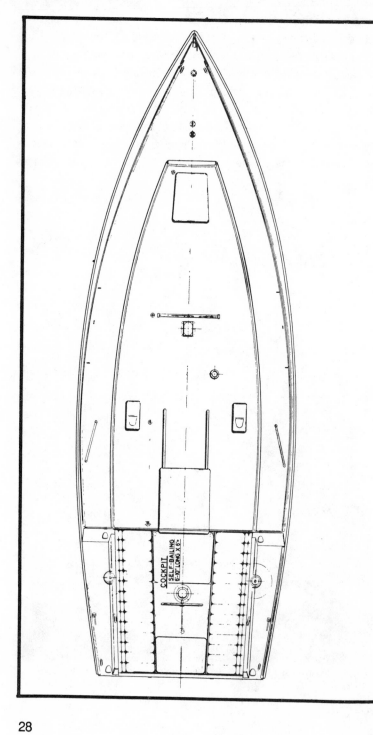

COCKPIT
SELF-BAILING
6'-10" LONG X 6'-

28

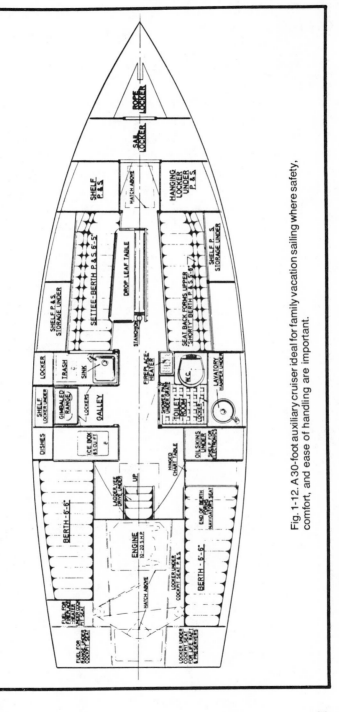

Fig. 1-12. A 30-foot auxiliary cruiser ideal for family vacation sailing where safety, comfort, and ease of handling are important.

the settees can be folded down to serve as beds for children. The drop leaf table offers plenty of room for comfortable dining. The navigator's area has a hinged chart table, a shelf for electronic equipment, and adjacent locker space. A fireplace-heater makes the cabin cozy and warm.

We have barely skimmed the surface in listing the types of boats at your disposal, but the sampling provided should at least point you in the right direction when you contemplate your next craft. How much you spend for labor, time, and materials is up to you, but by choosing wisely the type of boat best suited to your needs, you will insure that you and your family will derive the greatest possible enjoyment from your investment for many years to come.

# Basic Tools and
# Equipment for the Boatbuilder

High quality work in any trade or profession can be accomplished only by the correct use of high quality tools. The boatbuilding trade is no exception—even for beginners. Neat and accurate cuts must be made to insure tight-fitting joints; all joints must then be secured with the proper fastening devices; all surfaces must be finished for a neat final appearance. Superior results can only be obtained through the use of high quality tools kept in first-class condition.

People who have been building boats for a number of years have probably acquired a substantial array of fine power and hand tools capable of overcoming just about any problem that arises. The typical amateur boatbuilder, however, need not purchase such a large assortment of special tools. More than likely, the tools you now keep in your tool box or shop will be adequate for boatbuilding. The few special tools that will be required for your project can be borrowed or rented without the outlay of too much cash. You should also consider the use of one of the many boatbuilding centers that have been springing up all over the country in the last few years. These do-it-yourself centers not only offer the amateur boatbuilder the assortment of tools necessary for the construction of boats, but they also have experienced personnel available to give advice. All of this, of course, costs money, and a query will quickly tell you if the additional tools and advice are worth the price.

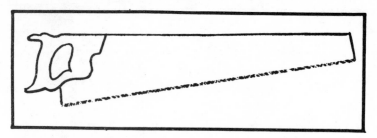

Fig. 2-1. For best results, a 5 1/2-point saw should be used at a 60-degree angle for ripping.

The tools commonly used by the amateur boatbuilder are described in this chapter. This list contains only the tools essential (in most cases) for doing good work on the usual kinds of boats attempted by the amateur boatbuilder. The tools should be of the highest quality the builder can afford, since they are certain to be used for many other purposes around the home. Bear in mind that high quality tools will last a lifetime.

## SAWS

Saws most often seen in boatbuilding shops include the following types: hand ripsaw, hand crosscut saw, keyhole saw, hacksaw, coping saw, and perhaps a bow saw. The most popular blade lengths for handsaws are 24 and 26 inches. Blades are categorized (fine or coarse) according to the number of cutting teeth (points) per inch. To illustrate, a coarse ripsaw 5 1/2 points per inch works fast and is excellent for cutting green wood. On the other hand, a fine saw with 10 or 11 points per inch is best for smooth accurate cutting on dry seasoned wood.

When purchasing any type of saw, look for blades of tempered spring steel or stainless steel. Blades of this type will hold sharp edges longer and are easy to sharpen; lower grade steel quickly loses its edge and is difficult to sharpen. Also look for blades with a rust-resistant or Teflon-S finish. Other desirable features in handsaws include: hardwood or sturdy plastic handles; screws rather than brass rivets securing the blade to the handle; greater thickness at the cutting edge to prevent binding; and cutting teeth set in alternate rows—one pointing right and the other left—to prevent binding by cutting a path wider than the blade itself.

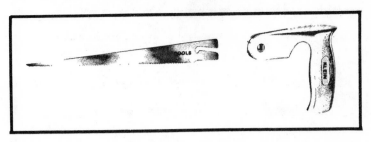

Fig. 2-2. A keyhole or compass saw is used to cut either curved or straightside holes.

For best results, a 5 1/2-point ripsaw should be used at a 60-degree angle (Fig. 2-1) to the board. The best cutting angle for a crosscut saw is approximately 45 degrees. You will find many uses for both of these saws when building any type of wooden boat, even though your shop has several power tools!

A keyhole or compass saw can be used to cut either curved (like a keyhole) or straight-sided holes. The blade is narrow and tapers rapidly to a point and can be inserted in the smallest openings. Several styles are available which will meet most of your cutting requirements (Fig. 2-2).

Coping saws cut irregular shapes and intricate patterns and consist of a steel frame and a narrow blade under tension (Fig. 2-3). Blades vary in shape and size from wire-thin to flat and 1/8-inch wide. They are removed from the frame in the same manner as a hacksaw blade.

Interior cuts, such as a hole for a drain plug in your boat, are made by first drilling a small hole (just large enough to admit the saw blade) and then threading the blade through the hole and attaching it to the frame clamps (or pawls). Some blades are made to turn in the frame, while others have the virtue of being able to cut in any direction regardless of the frame's orientation.

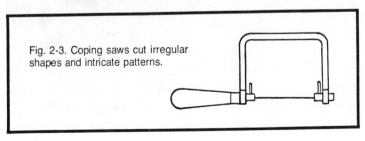

Fig. 2-3. Coping saws cut irregular shapes and intricate patterns.

33

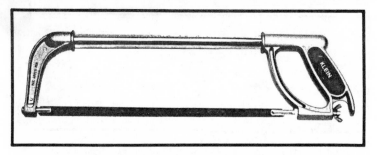

Fig. 2-4. The common hacksaw is used to cut metal of all types.

Everyone is familiar with the common hacksaw (Fig. 2-4) used for cutting metal of all types. Blades are available in a variety of designs for all types of cutting. The finest-toothed blades (32 teeth per inch) are used to cut extra thin materials, lightweight angle iron, wire rope, and cable. The medium blade (18 teeth per inch) is a good all-purpose blade suitable for cutting extra tough steel.

Frames vary in style and price, but all of them can be adjusted to accept different blade lengths. Some frames are designed for holding the blade in either a vertical or a horizontal position and some of the tubular frames store extra blades.

When deciding which blade to use for your application, a good rule of thumb is to have always at least three teeth in contact with the

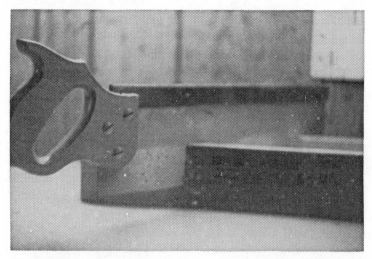

Fig. 2-5. A backsaw is a type of thin crosscut saw with a reinforced back to provide additional rigidity.

34

object you are cutting. This is especially true for coarse teeth since they have a tendency to snap when used on thin material, and with fewer than three teeth in contact.

A backsaw (Fig. 2-5) is a type of thin crosscut saw with a reinforced back to provide rigidity during the precision cutting of joints. The blades of the backsaw vary in length from 10 to 14 inches and in points per inch from 7 to 14. Backsaws are most commonly used with miter boxes (Fig. 2-6). This combination is a necessity for cutting neat and accurate angle joints.

If you find that your projects require the cutting of several circular holes in wood from, say, 1/2 inch to 4 inches in diameter, you may want to purchase a set of hole saws or circle cutters. Such saws feature a drill bit encircled by a saw blade and are sold as a nest of various diameters. They can cut a circular hole in a 2-inch piece of wood nearly as fast as a conventional wood drill could bore through.

Since all saws will eventually become dull with use, you should obtain some metal files and a tooth-setting tool to sharpen and re-position the teeth. Afterwards they'll be as good as new—if not better! When sharpening the teeth, only a few short forward strokes of the file are needed. Keep the same angle and let the brightening of the metal be your guide.

The tooth-setter (often called a saw set) is used to reset or bend the teeth back to their original positions to insure a cut that is wider than the blade, thus forestalling binding. A good saw set is designed so that the saw teeth can be seen during the setting process and it has all the calibrations necessary to insure an even set to each tooth. Such saw sets can be used on nearly every type of saw from the hand crosscut and ripsaw to the backsaw and on sizes from 4 to 16 teeth per inch.

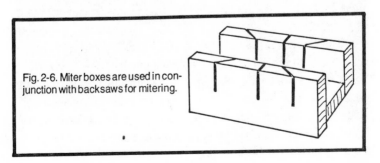

Fig. 2-6. Miter boxes are used in conjunction with backsaws for mitering.

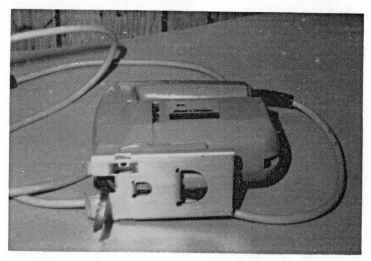

Fig. 2-7. The sabre saw is probably the most popular type of power saw for homeowners and handymen.

Portable power saws substitute electrical power for elbow grease, but you're still going to need those hand tools from time to time. Of the portable power saws, the sabre saw (Fig. 2-7) is the most popular among homeowners and handymen because of its low cost and versatility. The blades extend outward from the body, resembling the design of a keyhole saw, and the cutting action is obtained from the backward and forward movement of the blade.

The sabre saw is adaptable to an assortment of blades which enables it to cut soft and hard woods, plastics—even metals. The saw's versatility makes it an extremely practical tool for both the amateur boatbuilder and the general handyman. The sabre saw is unexcelled for scroll work, and is highly qualified for cutting plywood, boards, plastics, laminates, rubber, aluminum, brass, and steel. It can make pocket cuts, grooves and joints, and even create its own hole in soft woods.

The use of the sabre saw for long straight cuts, however, is usually difficult for the beginner, unless some sort of guide is used. Some sabre saws have their own adjustable guide bar. If your saw doesn't have this feature or if the span is too great for the adjustable guide bar, a strip of straight wood nailed to the board being cut will serve as a guide, the flat of the blade making constant contact with the strip during the blade's traverse.

36

Your second choice of portable saw would probably be a high speed circular saw. Most saws of this type are equipped with a rip guide for use on long pieces. Many models are designed to cast the sawdust away from the cutting line—a very helpful feature. A circular saw can cut a board much quicker than even the portable power sabre saw, but many boatbuilders find that this type of saw is not essential to their projects.

Power saws must be kept sharp—either by installing a new blade or by filing and setting the old one. Guards should be checked periodically to make certain that they are operating properly. The switch, plug, cord, insulation, etc., should be inspected for damage and wear. If the motor frame is made of metal, make certain that a grounding wire is attached and that the saw is never used except with a three-prong, properly operating plug.

Most of the fractional horsepower motors used on portable saws have sealed bearings that require no lubrication. Other frictional points should be lubricated with S.A.E. 20 motor oil. Use no more than 4 or 5 drops of oil at each point, first making sure that the mouth of each oil cup is clear.

Since all power tools are potentially dangerous, certain precautions should always be taken:

1. Make sure the switch is in the OFF position before connecting the power cord.
2. Never wear loose clothing that might become entangled in the tool's moving parts.
3. Disconnect the power cord before making adjustments on or changing the blade of a power saw.
4. Never operate a power tool in an enclosed area where gasoline or other inflammable or explosive substances are present.
5. Keep your fingers and other parts of your body away from the blade. If possible, keep both hands on the saw frame well away from the blade.
6. Make sure the tool is properly grounded. As an extra precaution, keep your hands and feet dry while operating the tool.

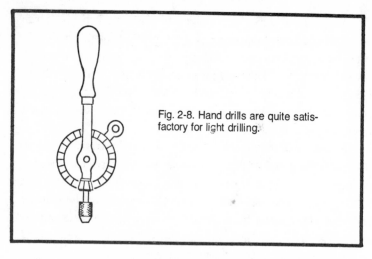

Fig. 2-8. Hand drills are quite satisfactory for light drilling.

7. When using long extension cords, make sure the wire size is No. 12 AWG or larger. Smaller wire can cause a voltage drop sufficient to damage the motor under hard use.

8. Switch off the saw motor immediately after making each cut.

9. Never remove a guard or other safety device from your power tool. One common practice which can have serious consequences is the removal of the third prong from the power cord plug—thereby eliminating the grounding protection.

10. Always wear glasses or goggles when operating power tools. One boatbuilder lost his sight when the blade on his saw broke and flew into his eye.

## DRILLING TOOLS

As a boatbuilder, you will find numerous occasions when a hole must be drilled through wood, plastic, or other material. For light drilling, hand drills like the one in Fig. 2-8 are quite satisfactory. This type features an adjustable chuck to permit easy exchange of bits in a range of sizes from 1/16 to 1/2 inch. The hand crank (operating much like an eggbeater) provides the drilling action via the train of speed gears.

Another tool for light drilling is the push drill (Fig. 2-9). Drilling action is accomplished by a push-pull movement in the manner of

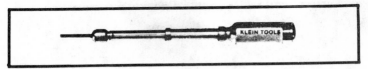

Fig. 2-9. The drilling action of a push drill is accomplished by a push-pull movement.

ratchet-type screwdrivers. Suitable for light usage, this tool is not recommended for heavy duty drilling. The boatbuilder will want to keep this handy drill in the boat's maintenance kit for use when electric power is not available.

A brace like the one in Fig. 2-10 is one of the older type drills but it is still widely used by professional carpenters, handymen, and others who need to bore holes of various sizes in wood. Besides guiding auger and drill bits, the brace can serve as a screwdriver when adapted with a screwdriver bit.

Drilling action is accomplished by turning the handle in a circular motion and bearing down on the head of the brace with the heel and palm of the hand. The head is mounted on ball bearings so that it will turn freely independent of the rest of the brace. Most of the better models also incorporate a ratchet control permitting the user to make half turns back and forth when there is insufficient room for a full circle.

Probably the most used hand power tool is the portable electric drill (Fig. 2-11). These useful tools are reasonable in price and find

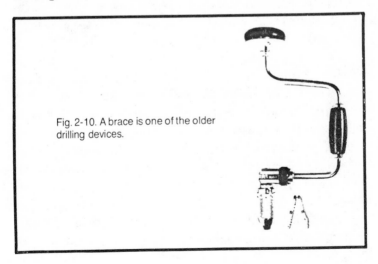

Fig. 2-10. A brace is one of the older drilling devices.

Fig. 2-11. The 1/4-inch portable electric drill.

many uses around the home and shop. The smallest of the conventional portable drills is the 1/4-inch drill. Such a drill has sufficient power for drilling holes in plastic, metal, concrete, and other materials when the proper bit is used. Many accessories—like a disc sander—are available for the 1/4-inch drill, making it an excellent tool for everyone to have around the home.

Single speed models operate at one speed only while variable speed (torque control) models offer the full range of speeds between zero and maximum. One model features 2-speed operation, high and low only. The method of changing speed differs according to the manufacturer, but the most common method is by means of a special trigger which controls the speed in response to finger pressure. Another model uses a dial control to vary the speed.

The next larger size of electric hand drill is the 3/8-inch. In addition to slightly larger chuck capacity, most of these drills are built with double-reduction gears to provide more torque and better operation at lower speeds. Some of these models are even equipped with reversible motors for backing the bit out of tight holes.

As mentioned previously, the many accessories available for both types of electric drills make them useful for many chores around the home or shop. Conventional accessories include a polishing wheel and pad, a wire brush, paint mixer, grinding wheel, sanding disc, etc. Also available are stands for securing the drill to a workbench or for use as a drill press.

Bits can be purchased in a wide variety of sizes and types. For example, your 1/4-inch portable drill can be used to bore holes in stone and concrete with a masonry bit and in all types of metal with metal cutting bits. Holes in wood may be drilled as large as 1 1/4 inches. The selection of the correct bit is of the utmost importance; it is a subject which could fill volumes. If you are in doubt about the appropriate bit for your project, consult your dealer.

There are several types of bits that you will find especially suited for speeding up your boatbuilding projects. One type is the countersink bit which widens the tops of holes so that flat head wood screws will fit flush with the finished surface. Expansion bits can substitute for larger or smaller bits because they can be adjusted by widening or narrowing the cutting blade to the required size. This is done either by a lock-screw or a geared dial. Twist drill bits are used in wood and softer metals to make clearance holes for bolts, screws, and the like.

## PLANES

Probably the next most important tool for the amateur boat-builder is the wood plane…a plane that is used for trimming, beveling, fitting and shaping wood, as well as for smoothing off rough spots left by saws and drills. Planes can be categorized into three general groupings: bench planes, block planes and special purpose planes.

Bench planes come in several different lengths from 8 to 22 inches and larger. The shorter lengths are used for all-around work while the longer planes with their greater cutting capacity are used for planing rough surfaces. The longer planes can also be used to shape the edges of boards so that close-fitting joints can be made.

A block plane like the one in Fig. 2-12 is the smallest and simplest plane. It is used in boatbuilding for smoothing limited areas and shaping small pieces of wood. Its single cutting blade sits at a low angle to the frame to permit better cutting. The height of the cutting blade can be adjusted by steel screws usually mounted on the end of the plane.

Special purpose planes include: rabbet planes used for cutting rectangular recesses in board edges or for incising grooves in any flat surface; circular planes for use on both concave and convex sur-

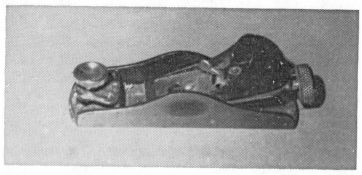

Fig. 2-12. A block plane is the smallest and simplest plane.

faces; and router planes for smoothing areas inaccessible to the regular planes.

It is unlikely that the amateur boatbuilder will have much use for any other kind of plane, but he should know that power jointer planers and conventional electric planers are available. The jointer planer is used to remove saw marks from battens and chines of boats and may also be used for fashioning rabbets and grooves. The electric planer can be used for fairing boats by first clamping a piece of aluminum (20 to 30 inches long) to the tool. With the aluminum serving as a straight edge, the planer can fair chines and battens very efficiently. Lengths of the aluminum used will depend on the size of the boat.

## SANDERS

In additon to a power saw and an electric drill, the boatbuilder will want to own an electric sander. Several types are available, but the orbital, or vibrating, sander (Fig. 2-13) will probably find the most use on home boat projects. This tool is lighter than most other sanders and its work is done by the action of a rotating sanding pad. The better quality orbital sanders can even do featheredging and flush sanding. The graduated series of sand paper available for this type of sander ranges from fine and extra fine to very coarse.

The vibrating-type sander will not remove as much wood in the same amount of time as the belt sander or some other types of sanders, but normally will give a smoother surface. This is especially true of the vibrating sanders which operate with a steady back and forth motion. Beginners can use their vibrating sander to achieve an extra smooth finish after first removing the rough surface with their 1/4-inch power drill and a sanding disc.

If you need to take off a lot of wood fast, then the belt sander is for you. This type of sander has a continuous belt with an abrasive (natural or artificial) surface which passes over drive cylinders at each end of the sander. The rear cylinder usually provides power—through a belt or chain drive—while the front cylinder free-wheels. A piston-grip handle on the rear of the sander enables you to push and pull the tool over the surface while a front knob will help you keep the machine level. The knob is equally useful for guiding.

This just about winds up the list of power tools you'll need for your boatbuilding project. Still, there are several other *hand* tools you'll need. A brief description of each follows.

## HAMMERS

Hammers are sized according to the weight of the metal head. Common purpose hammers are on the order of 13, 16 and 20 ounces. A good selection for all-around work would be the 16-ounce size. Either type of hammer, the curved claw (Fig. 2-14) or the straight claw, will suffice for your boatbuilding requirements.

Fig. 2-13. The vibrating sander will probably be the most-used sander on home boat projects.

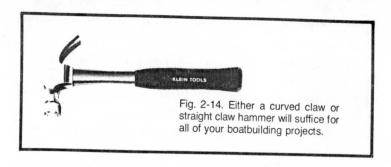

Fig. 2-14. Either a curved claw or straight claw hammer will suffice for all of your boatbuilding projects.

Mallets are selected according to the composition of the head: rubber, plastic, or leather. They are used to drive chisels and to close wooden joints where the blow of a metal hammer would mar the finish. The size of a wooden mallet (Fig. 2-15) is usually specified by head diameter, not by the weight of the head.

The hatchet is a combination tool which is part hammer and part axe. It is commonly called the carpenter's hatchet. It is excellent for removing a large amount of wood in a short period of time. Afterwards the rough surface can be planed and sanded to finish.

## MEASURING DEVICES

In boat construction, accurate measurements are absolutely essential. Fortunately, there are several easily-acquired devices capable of achieving the desired accuracy. These devices vary from simple folding rules to much more complicated instruments. For the amateur boatbuilder, however, a 6-foot folding rule, a measuring tape, and a steel square should suffice. Two of these measuring devices are shown in Fig. 2-16.

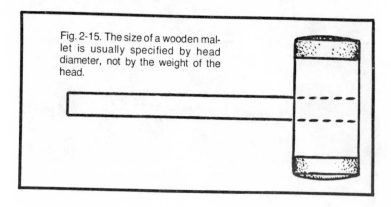

Fig. 2-15. The size of a wooden mallet is usually specified by head diameter, not by the weight of the head.

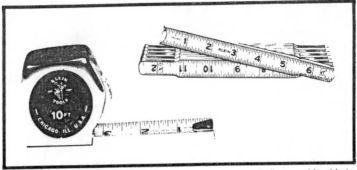

Fig. 2-16. A 6-foot folding rule and a measuring tape are indispensable aids to the boatbuilder.

## SCREWDRIVERS

Screwdrivers are available in a remarkable assortment of sizes, shapes and lengths. The quality of a screwdriver depends upon the quality of the metal in the blade, the method used for grinding the blade, and the manner in which the blade is secured to the handle. The composition of the handle is also a determinant in the quality of a screwdriver.

If its metal is of poor quality, the blade will easily chip and crumble under pressure. If the tip is improperly ground and flares too much, it will rise out of the slot while the screw is being driven. If the blade is not firmly attached to the handle or if the handle is made of a weak material, the blade will eventually work loose, or the handle will split and break. In either case, the screwdriver will be rendered useless.

The most common kind of screwdriver is the one used for driving straight-slotted screws (Fig. 2-17). The Phillips-head screwdriver (Fig. 2-18) has a cruciform tip for driving screws of a recessed, cross-slotted design. This type of screw is widely used for

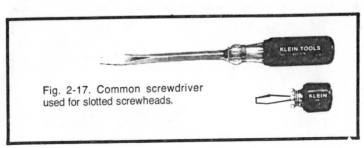

Fig. 2-17. Common screwdriver used for slotted screwheads.

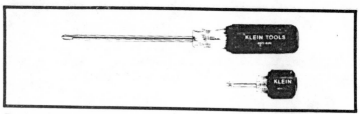

Fig. 2-18. The Phillips-head screwdriver has slots that cross at the center.

the trim and molding on larger boats. A Phillips-head screw reduces the chances that the driver will slip off the screwhead and scratch the finish of the board being worked.

Since most boat designs require dozens of wood screws to secure joints, the boatbuilder can save time and energy by acquiring a spiral ratchet screwdriver (Fig. 2-19). This type of driver has an adjustable chuck for interchanging various sizes of tips and even drill points. Ratchets can either drive or remove screws; converting from one mode to the other takes only an instant. Whether for entry or extraction, the operator need only press down on the handle.

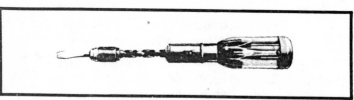

Fig. 2-19. Ratchet screwdrivers are great time-savers when many screws need to be driven.

Included among the other types of screwdrivers are the offset driver (Fig. 2-20) for use in places impossible to reach with ordinary drivers, and the spiral-bladed, screw-holding driver (Fig. 2-21) for starting screws in awkward spots.

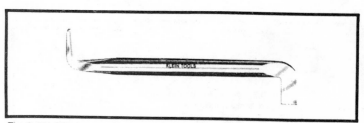

Fig. 2-20. Offset screwdriver for use in places where it is impossible to use an ordinary driver.

Fig. 2-21. Spiral screwholder blades are used to start screws in hard-to-reach spots.

## LEVELING DEVICES

Levels (Fig. 2-22) consist of a length of wood or metal fitted with a vial of liquid sealed in plastic or glass so that an air bubble inside the vial is centered when the level is sitting against a surface which is exactly horizontal (or vertical, if it is a dual-purpose level).

Fig. 2-22. Levels consist of a length of wood or metal with a vial of liquid sealed in plastic or glass and containing an air bubble.

## CHISELS

The two main types of chisels that will find use in boatbuilding projects are the butt and firmer chisels. The most popular, the butt chisel, has a short blade of 2 1/2—3 inches. Shown in Fig. 2-23, the firmer chisel is widely used for carving, paring, and similar work. It can be used with a hard-faced hammer.

A firmer chisel has a longer blade than the butt chisel and is used primarily for cutting deeply into wood. This type of chisel should be used only with a soft-faced hammer, such as a wooden mallet.

## CLAMPS

Clamps can be thought of as portable vises; they are absolutely necessary for most boatbuilding projects. In fact, you will probably

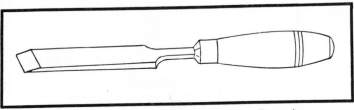

Fig. 2-23. Firmer chisel used for carving, paring and similar work.

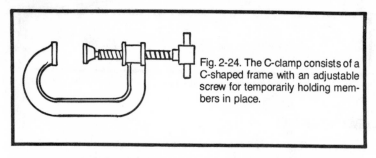

Fig. 2-24. The C-clamp consists of a C-shaped frame with an adjustable screw for temporarily holding members in place.

need several! They enable the builder to hold the objects he is working upon in any position and at any location. Clamps are often used to hold wooden joints together while glue is setting or until the builder can secure the joints with screws. The C-clamp and the bar clamp are the types most frequently used.

The C-clamp (Fig. 2-24) consists of a C-frame with an adjustable screw threaded through the lower jaw. These clamps are made of metal (iron or steel usually) and come in a wide variety of sizes and shapes. The size of a C-clamp is measured by its capacity: the dimension of the largest object the frame can accommodate with the screw fully retracted. The depth of throat or the distance from the centerline of the screw to the inside edge of the frame is also important. The smallest C-clamps have a 1-inch throat depth; the largest have a 12-inch depth.

Bar clamps consist of a bar or piece of pipe fitted with two flat-surfaced jaws. One or both jaws (depending on the type of clamp) can be moved along the bar's length to adapt to the size of the job. You can buy a bar clamp for holding 6-inch objects or one for

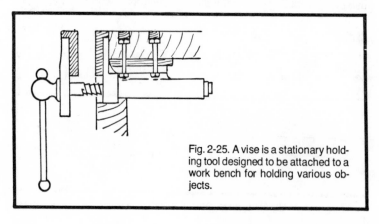

Fig. 2-25. A vise is a stationary holding tool designed to be attached to a work bench for holding various objects.

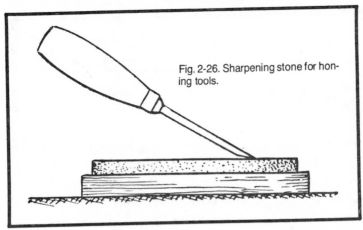

Fig. 2-26. Sharpening stone for honing tools.

holding 8-foot objects. Clasping pressure is applied by turning an adjustable screw installed on one of the jaws.

Other clamping devices include: the vise (Fig. 2-25), which is a stationary holding tool designed to be attached to work benches; the handscrew, which is basically two hardwood clamping jaws that are adjusted to the work by a pair of steel screw-spindles assembled into the jaws; the spring clamp, which is two metal jaws whose clamping pressure is obtained by the use of a steel spring; the band clamp, which is a fabric or steel band of suitable length that can be drawn tight around an object by turning a screw in the band-holding fixture; and the hold-down clamp, which is the screw portion of a C-clamp modified to secure to any surface.

## OTHER TOOLS AND MATERIALS

Other tools which you will find handy for your boatbuilding projects are sharpening stones (Fig. 2-26), files (Fig. 2-27), punches

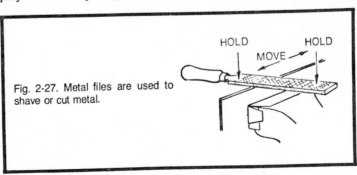

HOLD    HOLD
MOVE

Fig. 2-27. Metal files are used to shave or cut metal.

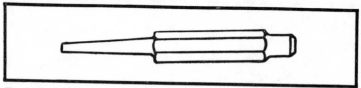

Fig. 2-28. Punches can be used for removing wood bolts and for many other purposes.

(Fig. 2-28), awls (Fig. 2-29), and nail sets. Perhaps you'll want an electric glue gun that uses sticks of glue melted by an internal heating element, the glue flowing out of the tip of the gun in a steady, even stream. This easy application makes glue guns popular not only with boatbuilders (who find that a great deal of gluing is required), but

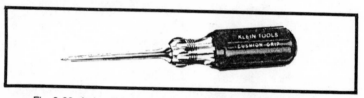

Fig. 2-29. Awls will find many uses around the boatbuilding shop.

with everyone from hobbyists to housewives for a variety of applications. The glue, which sets in 60 seconds, makes clamping unnecessary in most instances. Moreover, it will bond to almost any porous surface. The gun can further be used with sticks of sealer for applying water-proof caulking.

# Boatbuilding Lumber and Materials

Every professional boatbuilder knows where to get suitable materials...but what about the thousands of landlocked amateurs who are about to begin their first project? Where, for example, would a prospective builder in Kansas find sheets of marine plywood in 14-foot lengths, or Philippine mahogany for deck-work on cabin cruisers? He is probably going to find only 4' × 8' sheets of plywood at his local lumber yard; instead of Philippine mahogany, Douglas fir will more than likely be all that's available. To make matters worse, the local dealer—in most cases—will not even know where to order such materials!

There are hundreds of different boat designs and, if plans are purchased, the specifications may call for certain types of lumber you never heard of. In most cases, however, there are satisfactory substitutes. If this chapter doesn't answer all of your questions on wood substitutes, ask the workers at a large boatyard or a reliable lumber dealer. In lieu of this, write to the designer of the plans.

## PLYWOOD

Plywood is made of thin sheets of wood glued together in layers, with the grain of the top and bottom layers running in one direction, and the grain of the center core running oppositely. This cross-layering technique gives the wood strength and rigidity. Regardless of what part of the country you live in, you will get an identical product since all plywood is made to industry-wide specifications. Solid woods are not manufactured; by contract they are harvested in the forest, and sawed and finished at hundreds of different firms where the quality, hardness, strength, weight, and dimensions vary considerably. For this reason, the amateur will do well to stick to boat designs which strongly favor plywood construction.

Plywood comes in varying thicknesses, commonly starting with 1/4-inch and ranging up to 3/4-inch. It is normally sold in 4' × 8' sheets. Most plywood is made of Douglas fir. For boat hulls, many boatbuilders recommend the use of marine grade plywood, although for most projects attempted by the amateur boatbuilder, exterior grade A-B or better is cheaper and usually perfectly acceptable.

The difference between the two is that more care is used in selecting and matching the inner plies of marine plywood. There are no open knotholes or splits to collect the moisture which generates the rot that destroys the holding power of screw heads. When comparing marine and exterior (only) grades, you will note that the plies of the marine grade are carefully fitted together to eliminate the occurrence of voids between them. In contrast, voids are plainly visible along the edges of most sheets of exterior grade plywood.

A-B and A-C (or better) grades of plywood should be used on all members of the boat if marine plywood is not used. Any grade below A-C exterior plywood will almost certainly cause trouble in the future—even if it is used only as bracing in dry locations.

Even though plywood panels commonly are only available in the 4' × 8' size, sometimes 4' × 10' sizes can be found locally. However, any larger size will more than likely have to be ordered special. Panels longer than 10 feet are usually fabricated by splicing together two shorter lengths by means of a scarf joint. When properly mated, this type of joint is stronger than the original sheets, so there's no need for concern.

All plywood used in the construction of a boat should be finished sufficiently to avoid checking (parallel surface cracks). Adequate finishing is accomplished by first applying check-retarding plywood primer and then marine paint—not ordinary exterior paint, but real marine paint. The latter remains slightly elastic when dry and can flex in concert with the wood. The combination of primer and marine paint will inhibit checking and help your craft retain its good looks for the greatest length of time. Be especially careful to prime the ends and edges of plywood panels so that water cannot penetrate.

You are certain to encounter many sets of boat plans specifying the use of 1/4-inch plywood—mainly to obtain light weight in the craft. This thickness has proven satisfactory for light slow crafts like kayaks, plywood canoes, john boats and the like. However, for boats intended for higher speeds and powered by outboard motors, you may find this thickness unsatisfactory unless given further treatment. Even on the slower moving boats, the 1/4-inch thick hulls are easily cracked—if not punctured—if the boat glances off a rock in shallow waters or rapids. This thickness is also undesirable because of its tendency to show the ridges of the internal framing after the plywood has received a gloss paint coat.

Use of a thicker panel would preclude the disadvantages described above. A thickness something on the order of 5/16-inch—if available—would increase the overall strength significantly. If this thickness is not available, then 3/8-inch would be an adequate substitute. You should be aware, however, that this thicker plywood is very difficult to bend onto smaller vee-bottom boat frames where there is appreciable bend and twist in the bottom planking. In fact, on some designs like canoes and small dinghies, plywood as thin as 1/8- or 3/16-inch is required to achieve the necessary curvature.

There is a solution, however. These thin-skinned boats can be given extra strength and rigidity by applying a fiberglass covering. (Fiberglassing techniques are discussed thoroughly in later chapters.) This will, of course, add some weight to the boat, but the strength will be increased by two, three, or more times—depending upon the situation. Another solution is to use higher quality plywood panels. For example, normal Douglas fir plywood comes in three plies, while Philippine mahogany plywood—due to the uniformity of the grain and the absence of knots—come in five plies and is a much stronger panel. The additional cost of Philippine mahogany is substantial, but when extra strength is needed, it is well worth the price. The excellent appearance of such wood after finishing also makes it worth the additional cost to you.

## Solid Woods

If you're used to buying lumber in such common sizes as 1″ × 8″, 2″ × 4″, 2″ × 6″, etc., you're in for a big surprise when you shop at a boat lumber yard. Usually the lumber comes in random widths because the trees were sawed in a way to reclaim as many boards as possible. However, some boat lumber firms—like the M.L. Condon Co. of White Plains, N.Y.—will furnish you with exactly what you need. Just mail them your materials list with all the dimensions and they will rip and plane to your specifications, thereby saving you much time on your boatbuilding project.

Firms specializing in boat lumber, can supply fir and mahogany marine plywood in lengths up to 16 feet. They also offer such solid woods as Sitka spruce, Philippine mahogany, Honduras mahogany, red and white cedar, teak, cypress, oak, and pine. Most of these firms are specialists in all types and sizes of both domestic and imported boat lumber.

Another point about boat woods to consider is the method by which they are dried. Most of the wood found in your local lumber yard will have been seasoned by kiln drying, and can be expected to swell somewhat when used in boat construction. This should be of little concern to the amateur boatbuilder because most of his boats will be constructed of plywood—only the framing members will require solid wood. Nearly all of these members will be on the *inside* of a leakproof plywood skin and the slight swelling (caused by bilgewater) of bottom frame members will be of little consequence. However, it would be only prudent for the boat builder to use air-dried lumber when available.

A lumber's resistance to rot is of great importance in boatbuilding. Certain woods, because of their natural oil content, have greater resistance to rot. Both red and white cedar, for example, are highly rot-resistant. White oak also has excellent rot-resistance. Red oak, on the other hand, will rot quickly and should never be used for boat construction. Birch, even though a very hard wood, also rots quickly and therefore has no place in boatbuilding.

Wood rot is caused by a fungus which requires certain conditions to survive. Dry wood won't rot because it hasn't enough moisture to sustain the fungus, and waterlogged wood won't rot because it hasn't enough oxygen to sustain the fungus. Rot occurs only under warm, damp conditions.

The following list describes those woods that have been traditionally used for boat construction. All may be purchased from the M.L. Condon Co., 250 Ferris Avenue, White Plains, N.Y. 10603.

**White Oak** (*Quercus alba*). 47 lbs./cu. ft. Strong, tough, hard to split, holds fastenings very well.

**Long Leaf Yellow Pine** (*Pinus palustris*). 41 lbs./cu. ft. Heavy, tough and hard to work. High strength and good durability in water. Holds fastenings well. Frequently used for keels in pleasure boats and for both planking and keels in commercial construction.

Both of the above lumbers are especially suited for the construction of keels, frames, stems, knees, breast hooks, and other highly stressed parts of the boat.

**Philippine Mahogany-Dark Red** (*Pentacme contorta*). 38 lbs./cu. ft. A material of all-around suitability. Tough and strong, holds fastenings well, resists decay and finishes beautifully. Can be used for sawn frames, most structural members, plankings, trim, and joiner work.

**Honduras Mahogany** (*Swietenia macrophylla*). 42 lbs./cu. ft. A hard strong wood, easy to work, holds fastenings well, finishes beautifully. Suitable for any use on the hull of a boat in spite of its weight. The best material for joiner work in high quality yachts.

Both of these varieties are especially suited for planking, joiners, sawn frames, and most structural members and trim.

**Sitka Spruce** (*Picea stichensis*). 28 lbs./cu. ft. Light in weight and moderately strong, stiff, hard and tough. High strength to weight ratio. Because of this, and the fact that it can be obtained in long, clear, straight-grained pieces, it is the most popular wood for masts and other spars.

**Western Red Cedar** (*Thuja plicata*). 23 lbs./cu. ft. The finest of all the cedars. Light weight, easy to work, low shrinkage, high resistance to decay. Very popular for planking on small racing sailboats and other lightweight craft. Available in long lengths with clear vertical grain.

**White Cedar** (*Chamaecyparis thyoides*). Also known as juniper or as Atlantic, Jersey, or Southern white cedar. 23 lbs./cu.

ft. Light, smooth, easy to work, low shrinkage, high resistance to decay. Ideal for planking on small pleasure craft.

**Teak** (*Tectona grandis*). 40 lbs./cu. ft. Strong, heavy. Superior durability in water (possibly because of its oily nature). Because of its non-slip qualities, it is exceptionally good for decks when left unpainted.

## WOOD FOR BOAT DESIGN

The flat bottom design is commonly used for row boats, and occasionally for somewhat larger boats of design peculiar to certain localities. Flat bottom boats are usually less expensive than other types to build. Suitable woods for construction includes Southern white cedar, Philippine mahogany, and waterproof fir plywood. Occasionally, framing members will be made of oak or some other hardwood. The flat bottom is the easiest kind of a boat to build.

The vee bottom design is used for most high speed runabouts, cruisers and lower cost sailboats. Its broad popularity is largely due to ease of construction and first-rate performance qualities. Framing is usually of sawn oak; keel or oak of Philippine mahogany; planking of Virginia white cedar, Western red cedar, Philippine mahogany or waterproof plywood; decks of teak; cabins and trim of teak or Philippine, Honduras or African mahogany.

The round bottom design—either lap strake or smooth planked—is used for every type of boat from 8 to 100 feet or more. It is adaptable to almost any shape the designer can conceive. Although it is built from practically the same materials as the vee bottom, once the construction procedure is understood and equipment on hand, it is even easier. After the simple flat bottom skiff, the lapstrake and strip planked boats are the least expensive on the market. Unless he thoroughly understands the construction methods, however, the novice should not attempt this design for his first boat.

## LUMBER TERMS AND CONVENTIONS

To avoid the purchase of wrong material or sizes, the amateur boat builder should familiarize himself with the nomenclature used by supply firms. A list of standard lumber terms and conventions follows:

**Air-dried.** Lumber dried by stacking with space between the boards so that air can pass on all sides. Most boats are built of air-dried lumber. Air-dried lumber has a moisture content range of 9 – 18%.

**Kiln-dried.** Referring to lumber dried in a special forced draft oven or kiln that reduces the moisture content very rapidly and to a lower concentration than air drying. Since boats are always in a damp environment, kiln-dried lumber is seldom used.

**Green lumber.** Unseasoned or recently cut lumber.

**Square-edge.** Most lumber after being sawn in flitches is trimmed and its edges squared. Generally this is the most convenient type of lumber for constructing flat and vee bottom boats.

**Rough lumber.** Since a boat is usually built with boards of many thicknesses, boat lumber is sold in the rough or unsmoothed form and at the direction of the builder will be planed or dressed to the thickness required. Rough lumber (unlike dressed lumber) measures the full thickness stated and comes in quarter-inch graduations: 1/4", 2/4" or 1/2", 3/4", 4/4" or 1", 5/4" or 1 1/4", 7/4", 8/4", etc. The thickness of rough lumber is reduced by 3/16 inch as both sides are planed during the dressing process.

**Dressed or Planed lumber:** In regular lumber yards, all lumber is planed. When a board is referred to as being 1-inch thick, this means that the board was 1-inch thick before dressing. The planing operation will remove 1/8" to 1/4", leaving the purported 1-inch board between 3/4" and 7/8" thick (actual measurement).

**Vertical grain, Comb. grain, Edge grain, and Quarter sawn.** All terms are used to indicate boards sawn in such a way that the growth rings of the tree are approximately at right angles to the face of the board. In some woods, such as Western red cedar and yellow pine, this kind of sawing produces the most desirable boards from the standpoint of bending planks and finishing.

**Flat grain or Plain sawn.** Lumber sawn with the face of the board parallel to the growth rings.

**Flitch sawn.** Boards cut the full width of the log and left with the edges unsquared. White cedar is generally sold in flitches so that the builder in getting out a curved plank can take advantage of the full breadth as well as some of the sweep of the grain.

**Random widths and lengths.** Because of the select nature of boat lumber and the frequent need for the widest and longest boards possible, no board is trimmed to a stock width or length. Rather, just enough waste is removed to provide a clear, top grade board. It is conventional to buy and sell on this basis. Special or selected lengths and widths cost more. Currently the lumber mills will sell the long lengths only when purchased along with the short lengths. So please try to figure your order to include short lengths. There is great need for short lengths on every boat.

**Board measure or board foot.** A board foot is equivalent to a board 1 inch thick, 1 foot wide and 1 foot long.

Examples: 1″ × 6″ × 12′ 6 Bd. Ft.
1 1/2″ × 8″× 10′ 10 Bd. Ft.

Lumber less than 1 inch in thickness is considered to be 1 inch. The price of lumber is usually stated in dollars per 1000 board feet.

Using the proper wood in a particular boat design is very important, but equally important is the selection of the correct fastenings, glue, and other accessories.

### FASTENERS

In general, only two types of fasteners are suitable for boat-building: silicon bronze and hot dipped galvanized. Bronze screws should be used for all boats which will remain in salt or brackish waters for any length of time. It is recommended that *all* screws and other fastenings used in salt water boats be made of bronze. If this is not possible, at least use bronze fastenings on all joints below the waterline. For boats that will be trailered to and from the waters and not allowed to remain in salt water, hot dipped galvanized fastenings can be used. Most flat head wood screws come in sizes #8, #10, and #14 and lengths from 3/4 inch to 3 1/2 inches.

The best type of boat nail is the annular thread ring-type nail made of genuine bronze. These nails are normally packed in 1-pound boxes and come in lengths from 3/4 inch to 1 1/4 inches.

### BOATBUILDING GLUE

Plastic resin glue is recommended for making joints on all types of boats up to the largest size. It normally comes in a powder form for mixing with water. When used according to the manufacturer's instructions, the glue forms a bond stronger than the joining pieces. This type of glue, however, is not recommended for use with oak or teak woods when they will be subjected to salt water.

For use with any wood, resorcinol glue is considered to be the strongest and highest quality glue available for boatbuilding. When used according to the manufacturer's instructions, this type of glue forms a bond stronger than the wood members and is completely waterproof under all conditions of moisture and temperature. It comes in a two part powder/catalyst mix and has a working time dependent upon the ambient temperature.

## WOOD FILLERS

During the course of building any type of boat, you will need to fill various screw holes, dents, cracks, and other minor imperfections. One of the best materials to use is a plastic wood filler which applies like putty, dries rapidly, sands easily, and does not shrink; the last aspect is highly important. The filler should further be waterproof and weatherproof and have an oil-free base which can be painted over or covered with fiberglass cloth.

## MANUFACTURERS

The following list of manufacturers is furnished so that you can write them directly for any of your needs. Many have interesting brochures giving complete information on their lines of boat materials and accessories. Some of the complete catalogs may cost as much as a dollar or so, but the manufacturer will be sure to let you know of such charges before mailing the catalog.

## ANCHORS

**Anchormatic**
1020 E. 79th Terrace
Kansas City, MO 64131

**Bay Pattern Works**
Melan, OH 44846

**Danforth/White**
Portland, ME

**Herter's**
Rt. 2
Mitchell, SD 57301

**Sears Roebuck & Co.**
Philadelphia, PA 19132

## BILGE PUMPS

**Lovette Pumps**
Somers Point, NJ 08244

**West Products Corp.**
Box 707
Newark, NJ 07101

## BOAT CLOTHING

**Bristol Mfg. Corp.**
Bristol, RI 02809

**Charles Ulmer, Inc.**
City Island, NY 10464

**Commodore Uniform Co.**
349 Broadway
New York, NY 10013

**James Bliss & Co., Inc.**
Dedham, MA 02026

**Knee-Ease**
Box 156
Hingham, MA

**Outdoor Sportswear**
P.O. Box 905
West Palm Beach, FL 33402

**Seaboard Marine Supply Co.**
210 Montauk Hwy
Islip, NY 11751

**Superior Sports Specialties**
558 Library St.
San Fernando, CA 91341

## BOAT KITS

**Bay City Boats, Inc.**
Div. 5007
Bay City, MI 48706

**Folbot Corp.**
Stark Industrial Park
Charleston, SC

**John Wright, Jr.**
328 West Queen Lane
Philadelphia, PA 19144

**Luger Industries, Inc.**
3800 West Highway 13
Burnsville, MN 55337

**Riverside Canoes**
Box 5595-AG
Riverside, CA 92507

**Rodriguez & Nixon, Inc.**
Tanhouse Woods Rd
Hyde Park, NY 12538

**Snug Harbor Boat Works**
101-21 Snug Harbor Rd.
St. Petersburg, FL 33702

**Sportscraft**
Box 636P
Allentown, NY 08501

**Taft Marine Woodcraft**
636 39th Ave.
Minneapolis, MN 55407

## BOAT LUMBER

**M. L. Condon Co.**
246 Ferris Ave.
White Plains, NY 10603

## BOAT TRAILERS

**Herter's**
Rt. 2
Mitchell, SD 57301

**Holsclaw Bros., Inc.**
486 N. Willow Rd.
Evansville, IN 47711

**Sears Roebuck & Co.**
Philadelphia, PA 19132

## COMMUNICATIONS EQUIPMENT

**Communications Co., Inc.**
P.O. Box 520
Coral Gables, FL 33134

**Danforth/White**
Portland, ME

**Nova-Tech, Inc.**
1721 Sepulveda Blvd.
Manhattan Beach, CA 90266

**Pearce-Simpson, Inc.**
Miami, FL 33152

**Ray Jefferson**
Main & Cotton Sts.
Philadelphia, PA 19127

**RCA Sales Corp.**
600 N. Sherman Dr.
Indianapolis, IN 46201

**Servo-Tek Products Co.**
1086 Goffle Rd.
Hawthorne, NJ 07506

**Simpson Electronics, Inc.**
3635 S. Dixie Ave.
Miami, FL 33133

**Walco Electronics Co.**
9404 Ventnor Ave.
Margate, NJ 08402

## FIBERGLASS

**Herter's**
Rt. 2
Mitchell, SD 57301

**Sears Roebuck & Co.**
Philadelphia, PA 19132

## FIRST AID KITS

**Allan Marine**
325 Duffy Ave.
Hicksville, NY 11802

## FURNITURE

**Design Products Inc.**
1127 Goodrich Ave.
Sarasota, FL 33577

**Gold Metal Folding
  Furniture Co.**
1705 Packard Ave.
Racine, WI 53403

## HARDWARE

**Allan Marine**
325 Duffy Ave.
Hicksville, NY 11802

**Armco Steel Corp.**
Middletown, OH 45042

**BJ Marine Products**
Box 2709
Terminal Annex
Los Angeles, CA 90054

**Bunting Brass & Bronze Co.**
Toledo, OH 43601

**Gibb Yachting Equip. Co.**
1301 Folsom St.
San Francisco, CA 94103

**Gross Mechanical Prod.**
1530 Russell St.
Baltimore, MD 21230

**Johannessen Trading Co.**
5670 Wilshire Blvd.
Los Angeles, CA 90036

**Merriman, Inc.**
101 Industrial Park Rd.
Hingham, MA 02043

**Perkin Marine Lamp & Hardware Co.**
Miami, FL

**Powerwinch Corp.**
184 Garden St.
Bridgeport, CT 06605

**Research Enterprises, Inc.**
18 Stockton Pl.
Nutley NJ 07110

**Seaboard Marine Supply Co.**
210 Montauk Hwy.
Islip, NY 11751

**Sprague Marine Div.**
346 E. Walnut Lane
Philadelphia, PA 19144

**Star Marine Hardware, Inc.**
217 Sound View Rd.
Guilford, CT 06437

**T.E. Conklin Brass and Copper Co.**
115 Leonard St.
New York, NY 10013

**Wilcox-Crittenden Div.**
North & Judd Mfg. Co.
Middletown, CT 06457

### INBOARD MOTORS

**Barr Marine Products Co.**
2700 E. Caster Ave.
Philadelphia, PA 19134

**Chris-Craft Corp.**
Pompano Beach, FL 33061

**Cummins Engine Co., Inc.**
Columbus, IN

**Detroit Diesel Engine**
General Motors Corp.
13400 W. Outer Dr.
Detroit, MI 48228

**Holman & Moody, Inc.**
Municipal Airport
Charlotte, NC 28219

**J.H. Westerbeke Corp.**
35 Tenean St.
Boston, MA 02122

**Marine Dynamics Co.**
21-55 71st St.
Flushing NY 11370

**McCulloch Corp.**
6101 West Century Blvd.
Los Angeles, CA 90045

**Perkins Diesels, Inc.**
Box 500
Wixom, MI 48202

**Seamaster Marine Co.**
280 W. Sunrise Hwy.
Freeport, NY 11520

### KITCHEN EQUIPMENT

**Homestrand, Inc.**
Larchmont, NY 10538

**Marvel Industries, Inc.**
P.O. Box 327
Sturgis, MI 49091

**Morphy-Richards, Inc.**
128 Ludlow Ave.
Northvale, NJ

**Princess Mfg. Corp.**
741 S. Fremont Ave.
Alhambra, CA 91803

**Stow-A-Way Products, Inc.**
103 Ripley Rd.
Cohasset, MA 02025

**The Crow's Nest**
16 E. 40th St.
New York, NY 10016

## MISCELLANEOUS EQUIP.

**Cosom Corp.**
6030 Wayzata Blvd.
Minneapolis, MN 55416

**F.S. Ford. Jr.**
Naval Architects
93 Kercheval Ave.
Grosse Point, MI 48236

**Lands End Yacht Stores, Inc.**
2241 North Elston Ave.
Chicago, IL 60614

**Ray Jefferson**
Main & Cotton Sts.
Philadelphia, PA 19127

**Sudbury Laboratory**
Box 1166
Sudbury, MA 01776

**The Crow's Nest, Inc.**
16 E. 40th St.
New York, NY 10016

**The Standard Products Co.**
2130 West 110 St.
Cleveland, OH

**Trident Marine Prod.**
375 Park Ave.
New York, NY

## NAVIGATION EQUIP.

**Columbian Hydrosonics, Inc.**
Freeport, LI, NY 11529

**Danforth/White**
Portland, ME

**Decca Radar, Inc.**
386 Park Ave. So.
New York, NY 10016

**Karr Electronics Corp.**
2250 Charleston Rd.
Mountain View, CA 94041

**Kelvin Hughes America Corp.**
Box 1951
Annapolis, MD 21404

**Stanpat Products, Inc.**
Covert & Main Sts.
Port Washington, NY 11050

## OUTBOARD MOTORS

**Chrysler Outboard Corp.**
Hartford, WI 53027

**Evinrude Motors**
4087 N. 27th St.
Milwaukee, WI 53216

**Holman & Moody, Inc.**
Municipal Airport
Charlotte, NC 28219

**Johnson Motors**
Waukegan, IL 60085

**McCulloch Corp.**
6101 West Century Blvd.
Los Angeles, CA 90045

**Outboard Jet, Inc.**
1105 E. 54th St.
Indianapolis, IN 46220

## PAINT, EPOXY AND SEALANTS

**3M Company**
2501 Hudson Rd.
St. Paul, MN 55119

**Alroy Process Corp.**
37 W. 20th St.
New York, NY 10011

**C.A. Woolsey Paint&Color Co.**
201 E. 42nd St.
New York, NY 10017

**Defender Industries, Inc.**
384 Broadway
New York, NY 10013

**Dow Corning Corp.**
Box 7038
Greensboro, NC 27407

**International Paint Co., Inc.**
21 West St.
New York, NY 10006

**Petit Paint Co., Inc.**
Belleville, NJ 07109

**Samuel Cabot, Inc.**
195 S. Terminal Trust Bldg.
Boston, MA 02210

**Sav-Cote Chemical Labs**
P.O. Box 770
Lakewood, NJ 08701
         or
P.O. Box 78562
Los Angeles, CA 90016

## PLANS AND PATTERNS

**Cleveland Boat Blueprint Co.**
Box 18250
Cleveland, OH 44118

**Glen L Marine Designs**
9152 Rosecrans
Bellflower, CA 90707

**Marinecraft**
Box 161-T
Brighton, MA

**Outdoor Sports**
Box 1213-P
Tuscaloosa, AL 35401

## ROPE

**Puritan Mills**
Marine Div.
Louisville, KY 40222

## SAILS

**Bacon & Assoc., Inc.**
616 Third St.
Annapolis, MD 21403

**Chow's Trading Co.**
Box 529Y
Northport, NY 11768

**Clinton Johnson**
13185 49th St.
St. Petersburg, FL 33732

**Defender Industries, Inc.**
384 Broadway
New York, NY 10013

**Hild Sails, Inc.**
225 Fordham St.
City Island, NY 10464

**Hood Sailmakers, Inc.**
Little Harbor Lane
Marblehead, MA 01945

**Howe & Brainbridge, Inc.**
200 Commercial St.
Boston, MA 02109

**Thurston Sails, Inc.**
406 Water St.
Warren, RI 02885

## TOOLS

**Hans F. Geiger & Assoc.**
5845 N. New Jersey St.
Indianapolis, IN 46220

**The Black&Decker Mfg. Co.**
Towson, MD

**The Bunting**
  **Brass & Bronze Co.**
Toledo OH 43601

## WAXES, CLEANERS, ETC.

**Aladdin Products**
Huntington Sta., NY 11746

**Gary Marine Products Co.**
19818 Mack Ave.
Detroit, MI 48236

## WEATHER EQUIPMENT

**Aqua Meter Instrument Corp.**
Roseland, NJ 07068

**Danforth/White**
Portland, ME

# What About Boat Kits?

Do you ever dream of commanding a medium size sailboat, cabin cruiser, or even a small yacht but think prices are too steep for your budget? Perhaps you could afford one if you could build it from scratch; but with no other boat projects under your belt, you just can't see your way clear to tackle such a project at this time. There may still be an answer.

If you're willing to invest a week or two of assembly time, you can own the boat of your dreams at a fraction of the cost of a factory-built boat. If you have the average ability to accomplish odd jobs around the house and can use ordinary hand tools with average skill, then you can put together one of the many boat kits available on the market.

Boat kits are available in all shapes, sizes and types...from surf boards to canoes...from kayaks to fishing boats...from sailboats to cabin cruisers. With the majority of these kits, all the guesswork is eliminated; most of the hard work—like molding, cutting and fitting—is done beforehand by the manufacturer. All that is left for you to do is to assemble the pieces by following the detailed step-by-step instructions.

Since most of the parts in boat kits are precut and shaped, your finished craft will look exactly like a factory boat. Boats of the larger kits are designed by naval architects and styled by professionals, as are the most expensive factory built boats. Manufacturers of the kits claim that the owner-builder should save about one-half the cost of a comparable factory-finished boat. In other words, if you have a limited amount of money to spend on a boat, you can expect about twice as much boat for your money when you build from a factory kit.

Many people may look at a photograph of one of the larger kits and still have doubts about their ability to assemble such a boat. But if you have average mechanical aptitude and a desire to do-it-yourself, the manufacturers have carefully developed simplified step-by-step instructions to enable you to assemble any of the kits just like an old hand. In most cases, you won't need any help either. Even with the larger designs, you'll only need some assistance from one or two helpers while placing some of the bulkier parts (hull side sections, bottom, transom, etc.) in position. Once these parts are in position, however, you will be able to complete the assembly all alone, if you desire. Furthermore, you will need only a limited amount of space; your garage, carport, driveway, or back yard will do fine.

Many of these boat kits are also adaptable to the making of minor changes during construction. Although most manufacturers don't recommend making changes to the structure of the boat, or the shape or length of the hull, changes in the seating, cabin arrangements, and similar items can be made to suit yourself.

One of the largest manufacturers of boat kits is Luger Industries, Inc., 3800 West Highway 13, Burnsville, Minn. 55337. When you accept delivery of one of their boats, say, the 26-foot Tradewind shown in Fig. 4-1, the molded fiberglass hull and superstructure units will already have been joined together at the factory. The company also will have installed many of the bolts, a necessity for transporting the craft to the final place of assembly.

You will then complete the joining of the hull and superstructure units with stainless steel bolts and fiberglass bonding material supplied in the kit. The bonding process takes place entirely on the inside of the hull, the work being completely concealed on the finished boat.

The balance of the project will consist mainly of assembling the cabin interior's accommodations, installation of standing rigging, swing keel, deck hardware and other accessories. Only common household tools are needed and previous experience or special

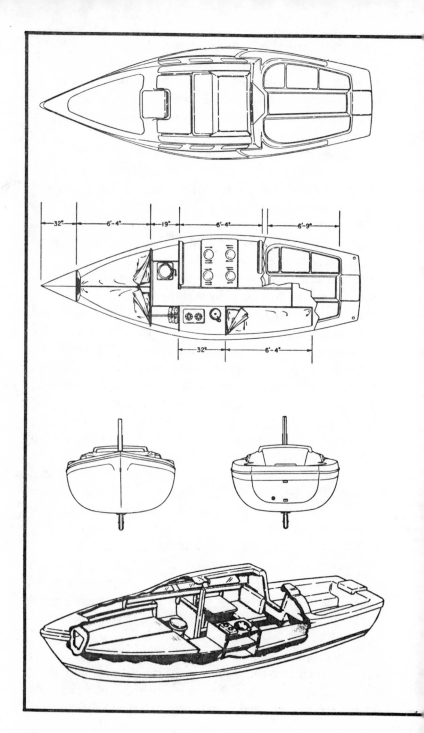

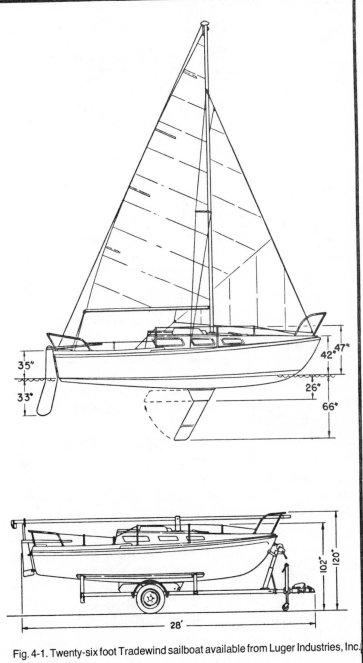

Fig. 4-1. Twenty-six foot Tradewind sailboat available from Luger Industries, Inc.

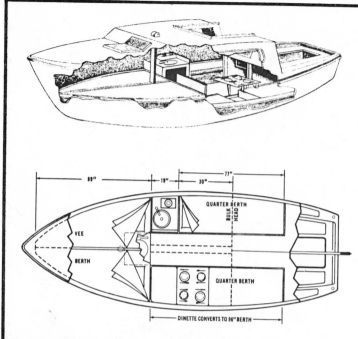

Fig. 4-2. Family cruising sloop available in kit form.

knowledge is not necessary—although these will make the job go a little faster. The entire project should be completed in about two weeks or 80 work hours.

Other kits by Luger include: the 21-foot family cruising sloop shown in Fig. 4-2; the 22-foot Caribbean cruiser (Fig. 4-3); the 22-foot Sport Fisherman (Fig. 4-4); and the medium size, easily transported, all-fiberglass sailboat shown in Fig. 4-5. This last craft could be launched within two weeks of the day you receive your kit!

If you haven't sailed before, you're in for new thrills and excitement. Just follow the simple sailing instructions included with every kit. Luger claims that you'll practically be an 'old salt' by the end of your first outing.

To illustrate how easy it is to assemble the factory-molded sections of this sailboat, read through these step-by-step instructions and see if you don't agree. Remember in doing so that this is a man size boat suitable for family sailing in winds up to 27 knots! This is not a toy.

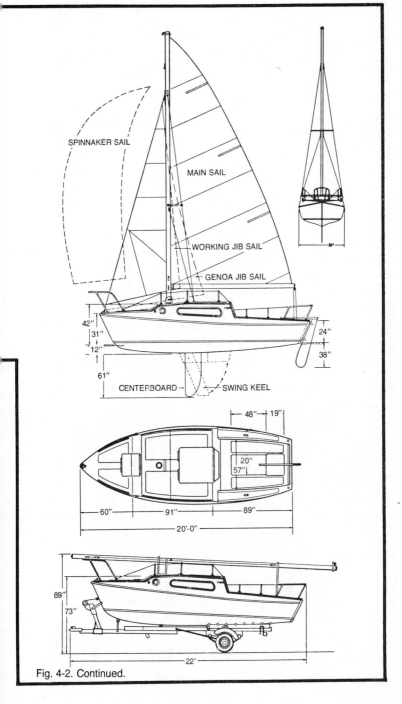

SPINNAKER SAIL

MAIN SAIL

WORKING JIB SAIL

GENOA JIB SAIL

42"
31"
12"
24"
38"
61"
CENTERBOARD — SWING KEEL

48" 19"
20"
57"
60" 91" 89"
20'-0"

89"
73"
22'

Fig. 4-2. Continued.

71

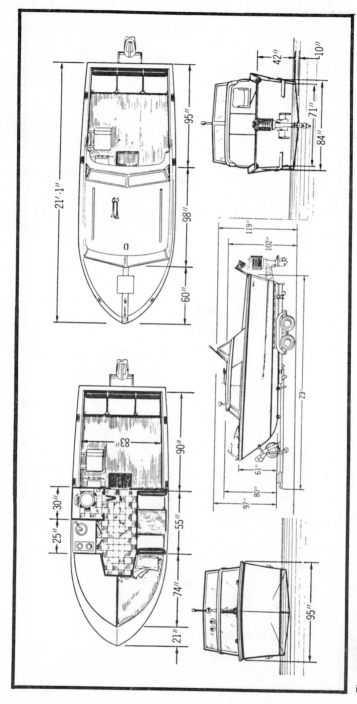

Fig. 4-3. Twenty-two foot cabin cruiser.

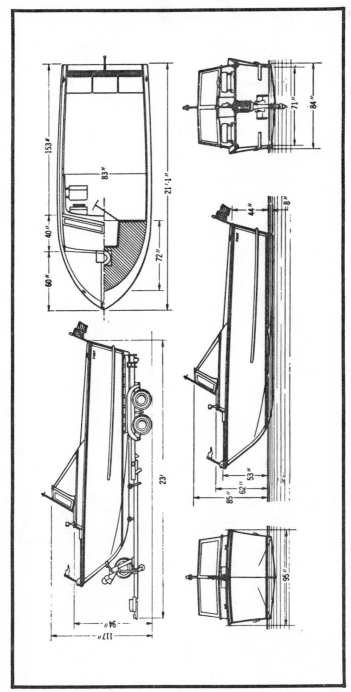

Fig. 4-4. Twenty-two foot Sport Fisherman.

73

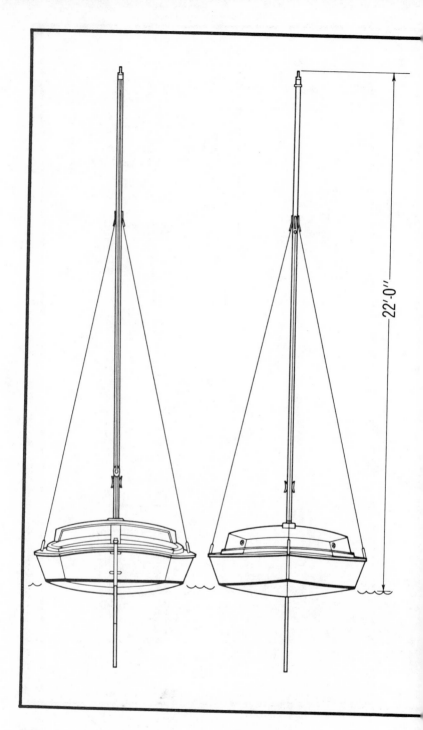

22'-0"

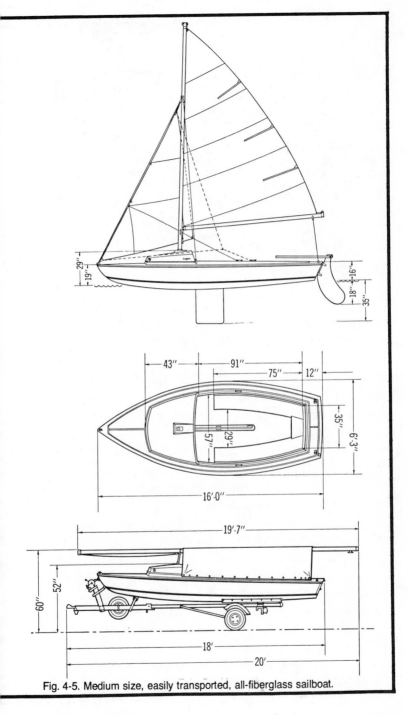

Fig. 4-5. Medium size, easily transported, all-fiberglass sailboat.

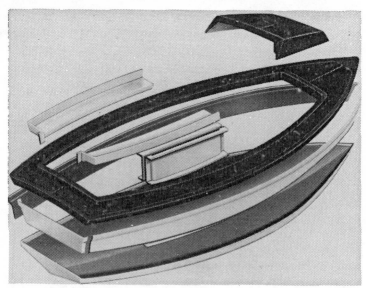
Fig. 4-6. Parts of a hull as contained in a kit.

The illustration in Fig. 4-6 shows the parts of the hull in an "exploded" view. All parts are fashionied from the finest seaworthy materials available and are designed to fit together, stay together, and require minimum maintenance. The manufacturer assures the builder that the Leeward has been carefully designed for easy assembly and carefree use, from the smallest screw to the permanent color-molded deck.

When your kit arrives, the parts will look something like the photo (Fig. 4-7). Here the builder is assembling the factory-molded fiberglass sections of the centerboard well with waterproof seam composition, brass screws and other pre-cut parts supplied with the kit. When completed, the centerboard well is fastened to the molded hull bottom with stainless steel screws.

Using an ordinary paint brush and working on a piece of scrap cardboard, saturate strips of fiberglass matt with polyester resin (Fig. 4-8) and add hardener. This and all other materials necessary to complete construction are supplied with the kit.

Bond the centerboard well assembly and the wooden hull reinforcing members to the hull interior with the saturated fiberglass matt strips as shown in Fig. 4-9. The resin quickly fuses and permanently bonds these members to the molded fiberglass bottom.

Fig. 4-7. Assembling the centerboard well with factory-molded fiberglass sections.

Fig. 4-8. Saturating strips of fiberglass matt with polyester resin.

Fig. 4-9. Bonding the centerboard well assembly and the wooden hull reinforcing members to the hull interior using the saturated fiberglass matt strips.

Next, slip the molded fiberglass side panels into place (Fig. 4-10) and fasten to bottom section using the small stainless steel screws supplied in kit. Two people will be helpful at this point. Interlocking flanges of the molded sections assure a perfect fit so you cannot go wrong.

Slip the transom into place by letting the interlocking flanges on sides and bottom guide it to a perfectly matching position (Fig. 4-11). Secure the transom with the stainless steel screws supplied. Then bond the joints and seams between boom, sides, and transom by using the bonding procedure described previously.

It will again take two of you to lower the molded fiberglass deck section into place as shown in Fig. 4-12. The flanges of this deck section match the transom and side flanges for a perfect fit. Join the deck to the transom and sides with stainless steel screws as before.

Fig. 4-10. Slipping molded fiberglass side panels into place.

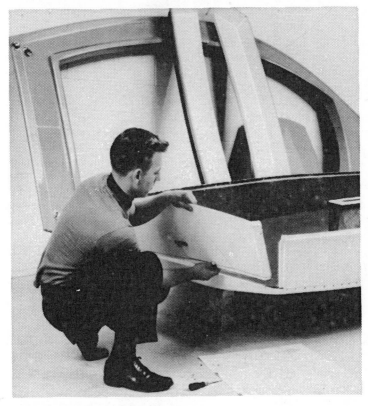

Fig. 4-11. Easing the transom into place.

Fig. 4-12. Lowering the molded fiberglass deck section into place.

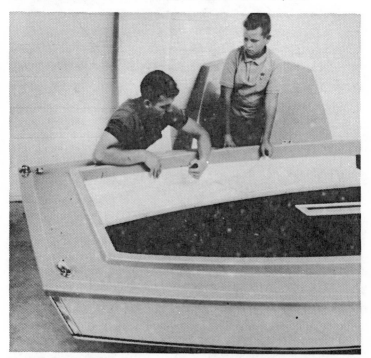

Fig. 4-13. The fiberglass seats are shown here in place and fastened with screws to the cockpit coaming.

Then bond with fiberglass along the out-of-sight interior side for a neat finish.

Slip the factory molded fiberglass seats into place and fasten with screws to the cockpit coaming (Fig. 4-13). Seats for this craft have comfortably contoured back rests and molded-in non-slip surfaces.

Again with the assistance of a helper, lower the fiberglass cabin top into position as shown in Fig. 4-14. Fasten this cabin to the deck section with stainless steel screws. These screws, like all screws fastening molded sections, should be countersunk, the depressions filled with putty and concealed with painted trim stripe or aluminum molding.

Now all the hard work is over. Complete your craft by assembling the rudder and dropping it into place on the transom. Slip in the centerboard, install the hardware, step the mast on the cabin top and then...launch her and sail away (Fig. 4-15).

Fig. 4-14. Lowering molded fiberglass cabin top into position.

Fig. 4-15. Launch her and sail away!

So in less than two weeks' time anyone can assemble this all-fiberglass sloop or any similar kit for that matter. Simply slip the precise, factory-molded sections together and then bond them into a seamless one-piece craft.

You'll find the mini cabin ideal for stowing gear when a light rain is present. A couple of air mattresses will also permit two people to camp out overnight with a solid roof over their heads. During chilly nights, the cabin offers enough protection for a small Coleman heater to keep you warm and comfortable. It's even warmer if a canvas tarp is thrown over the opening.

Have you ever had the desire to take the helm of a $12,000 to $14,000 cabin cruiser, but know that it costs just too darn much money for you at the present time? If you want to try your hand at assembling one of the kits on the market—like one of those furnished by Clark Craft, 16-1 Aqua Lane, Tonawanda, N.Y. 14150—your dream could come true sooner than you've imagined. Take the 26-footer in Fig. 4-16 for example. You can purchase the basic kit with all parts and members pre-cut for around $2500. Add another $5000 for inboard engine and accessories and you have a $14,000 express cruiser for less than $8000.

If you still think this is a lot of money for a recreation boat, take a look at the cutaway drawing in Fig. 4-17. Here you have two forward berths, a built-in galley, dinette area, head, and plenty of storage room—facilities enough, in fact, for a 1500 mile cruise. And since you're building the craft yourself, you can add or delete as many accessories as you desire.

When you order one of these kits from Clark Craft, either Mr. Clark or Ted Jones will suggest that you read through carefully all of the instructions before attempting to assemble your kit. You might even want to read through the instructions once, then go through them again while referring to the drawings. This will help you to familiarize yourself with the various parts in regard to their location in the hull.

Remember that the final appearance of your boat will depend on the finish you produce, so when you unpack your kit, it would be a

Fig. 4-16. Luxury cabin cruiser built from a kit.

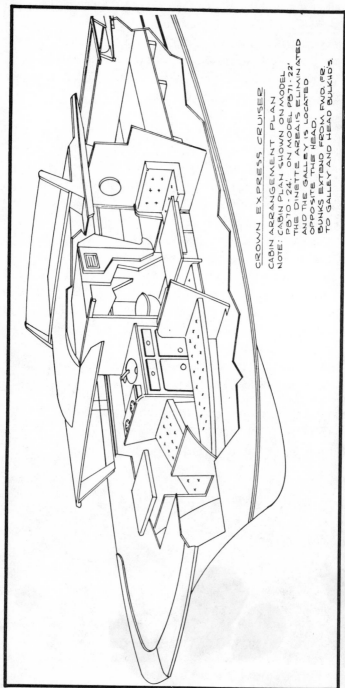

CROWN EXPRESS CRUISER

CABIN ARRANGEMENT PLAN
NOTE: CABIN PLAN SHOWN ON MODEL
P670-24: ON MODEL P671-22'
THE DINETTE AREA IS ELIMINATED
AND THE GALLEY IS LOCATED
OPPOSITE THE HEAD.
BUNKS EXTEND FROM FWD. FR.
TO GALLEY AND HEAD BULKHDS.

Fig. 4-17. Cutaway drawing of the cabin cruiser showing the arrangement of the interior.

good idea to sand and round all edges of the mahogany parts in the event you plan to varnish these later. A plywood sealer and finish coats of paint may be applied to the interior of the planking at this time if you desire.

In setting up the framework, be sure the surface on which you are working is flat and level along the entire length of the hull. Irregularities in the surface will transmit the same unevenness to your completed framework and you certainly don't want this in a $14,000 boat. The surface can be corrected by setting up a simple 2 × 4 jig and leveling it along its length and width. When this is done, establish a centerline on the floor or jig, whichever is used.

Refer to the drawing in Fig. 4-18 while measuring and marking a centerline on each frame crossbrace. Then take the girders (part #13) and cut out the notches marked in pencil. The factory leaves these uncut to prevent the possibility of these members breaking or splitting in transit. You can cut them out with a sabre saw or else you can run a hand saw down each side to the bottom mark and knock out the stock with a wood chisel. Clean up any rough edges by sanding.

Your next step would be to interlock frames #2, 3, 4, 5, 6 and 7 with the girders by placing them temporarily on the centerline of the floor or jig. Then assemble transom (part #10) as indicated in Fig. 4-20. You should place the parts in place before applying glue to familiarize yourself with the correct procedure. This also lets you know whether any parts are missing. Continue by fastening the center transom knee (part #11) as indicated in the sketch in Fig. 4-18. Be sure to keep this flush with the top and aft edges of the girder. Then fasten with three 1/4" × 3" bolts and glue in position for additional strength.

Fasten the inner keel part (#9) to the stem part (#8) by applying bedlast to notch in stem and fasten by drilling and inserting three 1/4" × 4" bolts. Clamp keel in position temporarily in the center transom notch. Butt the aft edge of girder and knee to the transom before clamping the braces temporarily on each side of the transom until the correct height has been obtained. The angle of the knee establishes the correct transom angle so you shouldn't have any trouble here. Fasten the keel at the transom notch by driving two 2 1/4-inch screws. Then apply bedlast to the keel notches.

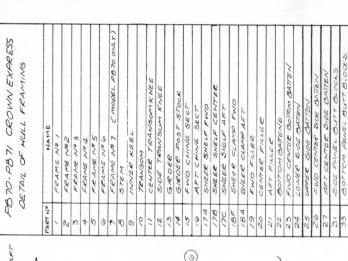

PB70-PB71 CROWN EXPRESS
DETAIL OF HULL FRAMING

| PART N° | NAME |
|---|---|
| 1 | FRAME N° 1 |
| 2 | FRAME N° 2 |
| 3 | FRAME N° 3 |
| 4 | FRAME N° 4 |
| 5 | FRAME N° 5 |
| 6 | FRAME N° 6 |
| 7 | FRAME N° 7 (MODEL PB70 ONLY) |
| 8 | STEM |
| 9 | INNER KEEL |
| 10 | TRANSOM |
| 11 | CENTER TRANSOM KNEE |
| 12 | SIDE TRANSOM KNEE |
| 13 | GIRDER |
| 14 | GIRDER POST STOCK |
| 15 | FWD CHINE SECT |
| 16 | AFT CHINE SECT |
| 17A | SHEER SHELF FWD |
| 17B | SHEER SHELF CENTER |
| 17C | SHEER SHELF AFT |
| 18F | SHEER CLAMP FWD |
| 18A | SHEER CLAMP AFT |
| 19 | FWD FILLER |
| 20 | CENTER FILLER |
| 21 | AFT FILLER |
| 22 | BOTTOM BATTENS |
| 23 | FWD CENTER BOTTOM BATTEN |
| 24 | LOWER SIDE BATTEN |
| 25 | UPPER SIDE BATTEN |
| 26 | FWD CENTER SIDE BATTEN |
| 27 | AFT CENTER SIDE BATTEN |
| 31 | SIDE PANEL BUTT BLOCKS |
| 33 | BOTTOM PANEL BUTT BLOCKS |

SHEET N°1   DWG. N° 63/00

Fig. 4-18. Detail of hull framing.

AFT

FWD

FE.3

BASE LINE   FE 2   FE 1

GLUE GIRDER POST

GLUE KNEES IN POSITION FOR ADDITIONAL STRENGTH

GIRDER

CHINE

NOTCHES TO LOCATE FILLERS.

GLUE SHELF WITH 3 FASTEN WITH 3 SIDE SCREWS AT EACH SIDE. PLACE SPACE BENEATH SHELF AT BOW END UNTIL—

86

From center point at keel notch measure 18 inches out on each side and mark the bottom edge of the transom. The girder will center on this mark. Fasten by driving two 1/4″ × 5″ bolts through transom board and the knee and then glue for additional strength.

Since the keel is straight from approximately the #2 frame to the transom, it would be a good idea to clamp a straight length of 2″ × 6″ board (on edge) to the keel to insure that this member will remain straight as you proceed to anchor framework to the jig or floor. After this has been accomplished, center the transom on centerline and anchor the braces to the jig or floor. Check to make sure that the transom angle is at the correct 75 degrees before centering the stem on the centerline and anchoring to the jig or floor. Fasten at aft edge as sheer shelf will be positioned beneath stem at forward edge.

Fit frame #1 (Fig. 4-18) in position first, and then the remaining frames. Fasten all frames with 2 1/4-inch screws and glue. Make certain that the forward edge of the frame and the forward edge of the keel are flush. Also, in anchoring the frame to the jig or floor, check to see that each frame is plumb, affixed to the centerline, and square with the centerline. In the event of any irregularities, use a shim to make certain that the frame is sitting solid.

Fasten girders to frames by driving one 2 1/4-inch screw at each notch. This screw should be countersunk enough so that you will not strike it when you plane it later. For additional bracing cut girder post stock (part #14) and fasten in position diagonally at each frame. Then secure with glue and 1 1/4-inch screws as shown in the sketch (Fig. 4-18).

Continue the framing by fastening together chine sections #15 and #16 at the scarf joint with glue and three 1 3/4-inch screws at each edge—countersunk enough to allow planing to correct bevel when fairing for the planking later on. Then locate the dimension on the stem and fasten in chine, parts #15 and 16. Make sure you select the correct one, right and left. Fasten at stem and frames with two 1 3/4-inch screws at each point. The beveled edge should rest on cheek of stem. Trim off excess at transom notch and check the frame dimensions on each side to insure identical spacing. Glue scarf joints and assemble the forward, center and aft sections (part #17A, B & C) of the sheer shelf as shown in the sketch in Fig. 4-18.

Fasten in sheer shelf at stem and at sheer notch of frame #1 and trim to fit. Nail frame crossbrace to jig at this time and then fasten in place at the stem with one 1 3/4-inch screw at an angle through the shelf into the stem and with two 2 1/4-inch screws through aft face of the frame into the shelf. For additional reinforcement at the stem, screw a small block onto the stem and shelf. After the hull has been turned over permanently, fasten the block to the stem with three additional 2 1/4-inch screws. Also fasten the forward sheet clamp (part #18) to notch in the sheer shelf with three 1 3/4-inch screws—bending these into position at the notches to achieve a smooth fair line at the sheer. If necessary, cut away portions of the clamp at the notches before fastening the clamp to the stem with one 1 3/4-inch screw at each notch.

Fit and fasten the forward, center, and aft hull fillers (parts #19, 20 and 21) in the approximate positions shown on the drawing (Fig. 4-18). Secure with wood screws through chine into filler notch and with one 1 3/4-inch screw through filler into sheer shelf. Forward and center fillers fasten at stem while the aft filler fastens midway between forward fillers and frame #1. The notches in the shelf are located at the bottom as shown in the drawing.

Next come the bottom battens (#22), extending from frame #2 aft to the transom. Secure these battens with 1 1/4-inch wood screws at each notch and then cut limber holes for water drainage as shown in Fig. 4-20. Check dimension of the stem and fasten the forward center bottom batten (#23) which extends from stem to frame #4. This batten is fastened in the same manner as the others.

Continue with the side battens (Fig. 4-18), and the butt block stock (#31 and #33). Then fasten the side transom knee (#12) to the chine and transom. The hull framework has now taken a general shape, but it still must be faired to receive the planking. Take a flexible batten and check the bottom framework by bending the batten from keel to chine. Trim off any high spots that will hold the planking away from the framework. This operation is very important, so take your time and do a thorough job. Then treat the side framework in a similar manner. It would also be a good idea to paint the edges of the frames before applying the planking, because this is the only time these edges will be open to receive any protection against moisture and decay. A coat of sealer applied to the inside of

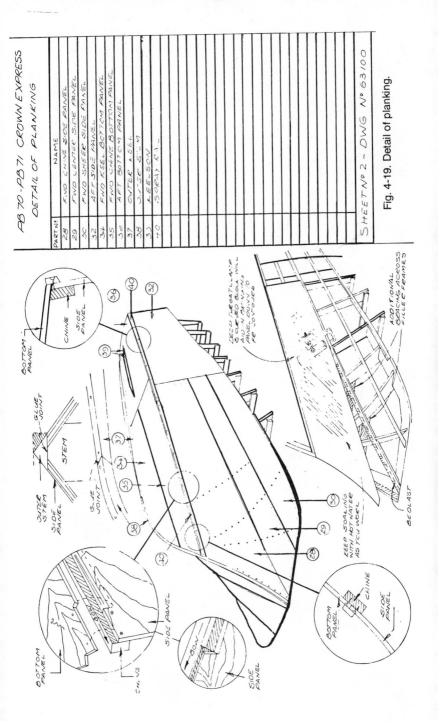

PB 70-PB 71 CROWN EXPRESS
DETAIL OF PLANKING

| PART N° | NAME |
|---|---|
| 28 | FWD CHINE SIDE PANEL |
| 29 | FWD CENTER SIDE PANEL |
| 30 | FWD SHEER SIDE PANEL |
| 32 | AFT SIDE PANEL |
| 34 | FWD KEEL BOTTOM PANEL |
| 35 | FWD CHINE BOTTOM PANEL |
| 36 | AFT BOTTOM PANEL |
| 37 | OUTER KEEL |
| 38 | OUTER STEM |
| 39 | KEELSON |
| 40 | (SPRAY) RL |

SHEET N° 2 – DWG N° 63100

Fig. 4-19. Detail of planking.

89

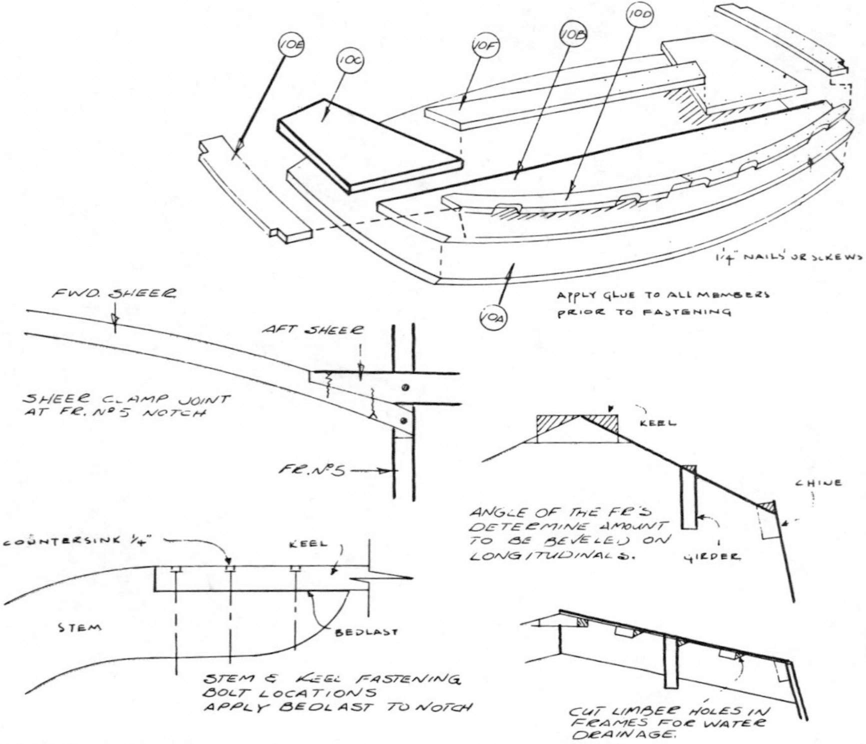

| PB70-PB71 CROWN EXPRESS TRANSOM DETAIL ||
| PART N° | NAME |
| 10A | TRANSOM PANEL |
| 10B | TRANSOM BOTTOM DOUBLER |
| 10C | TRANSOM SIDE DOUBLER |
| 10D | TRANSOM BOTTOM FR |
| 10E | TRANSOM SIDE FR |
| 10F | TRANSOM MOTOR PAD |

SHEET N°3   DWG. N°63/00

Fig. 4-20. Drawing of transom details.

APPLY GLUE TO ALL MEMBERS
PRIOR TO FASTENING

1¼ NAILS OR SKEW?

CHINE

KEEL

ANGLE OF THE FR'S
DETERMINE AMOUNT
TO BE BEVELED ON
LONGITUDINALS.

GIRDER

CUT LIMBER HOLES IN
FRAMES FOR WATER
DRAINAGE.

FWD SHEER

AFT SHEER

FR. N°5

SHEER CLAMP JOINT
AT FR. N°5 NOTCH

KEEL

BEDLAST

STEM & KEEL FASTENING
BOLT LOCATIONS
APPLY BEDLAST TO NOTCH

COUNTERSINK ¼"

STEM

the planking at the frame positions wouldn't hurt anything either. All of the planking details are shown in Fig. 4-19.

Once the planking is applied, fasten the other wooden members, like the keel, spray rail, etc., and then fill all screw holes and joints with a wood filler or fiberglass putty. Paint a coat of primer on the hull first; and if you want to obtain a smooth finish, a thin coat of glazing compound may be spread on the side planking with a broad knife. This will conceal any wavy grain in the ply. Sand smooth with a vibrator sander.

You should put a prime coat over the entire hull at this time. When this coat has dried, pencil on the water line and mark off a 1-inch boot top. Later, after the decking (Fig. 4-21) and cabin have been installed, apply two coats of bottom paint and a finish coat of white or color on the side. A boot top of contrasting color is normally recommended. If the hull is to be fiberglassed, however, it would be better now to leave off the outer spray rails so that the joints can be covered more easily later.

Turning the hull over is going to be one of the toughest jobs of the entire project, so get as many of your friends and neighbors as you can for help. A block and tackle at each end—securely fastened to the sheer and anchored to any ceiling beam or cross tie—will help ease the hull slowly over. It might be a good idea to fasten additional bracing at mid-point on frames inside the hull. To reduce the clearance problem, the tap extension of frames may be cut off flush with the sheer.

After the hull has been positioned for work on deck and cabin (see Fig. 4-22), level and block it up in several places so that it will not move out of place while you are fastening in additional bracing. The height of the hull from the outer keel to trunk top is approximately 6 1/4 feet, so allow enough headroom to remove the hull after the cabin has been erected. If you intend to install the optional flying bridge windshield, this will add another 20 inches to the overall height.

To prepare the hull for deck framing, trim the frames and stem extensions flush with the sheer line and remove any transom bracing. Trim excess planking flush with sheer also. It would help to construct a simple plank catwalk along the side of the hull at a convenient working height. Next, plane the sheer to a smooth fair

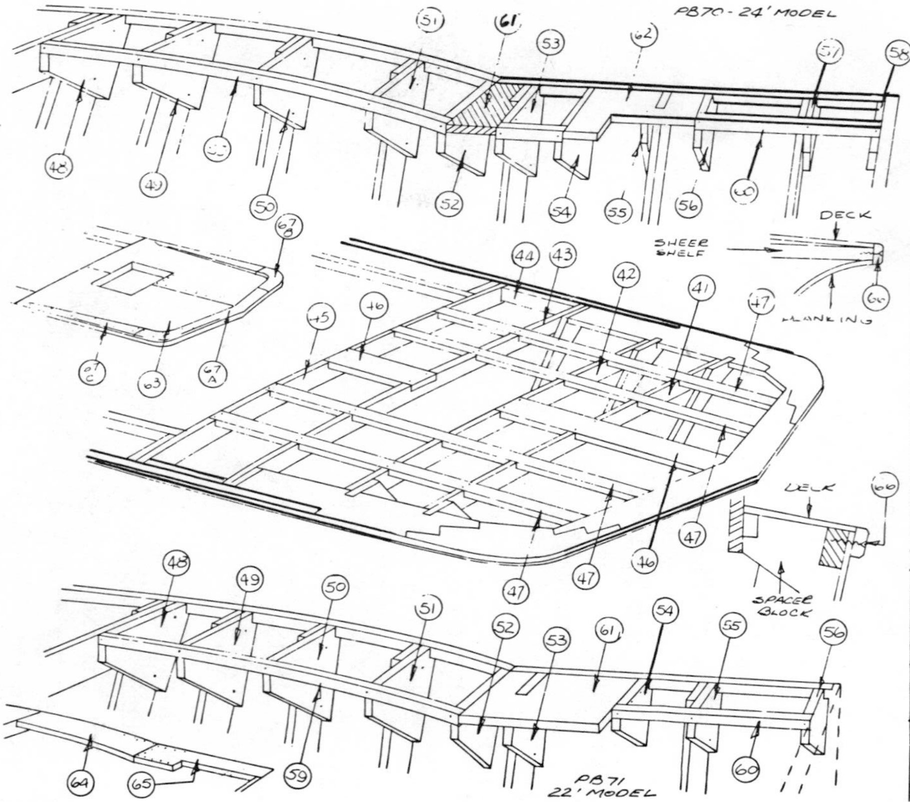

PB70-71 CROWN EXPRESS
DETAIL OF DECK FRAMING

| PART Nº | NAME |
|---|---|
| 41 | DECK BEAM Nº1 |
| 42 | DECK BEAM Nº2 |
| 43 | DECK BEAM Nº3 |
| 44 | DECK BEAM SPACE |
| 45 | DECK BEAM Nº4 |
| 46 | CENTER STRONGBACK |
| 47 | SIDE STRONGBACK |
| 48 | SPACER BLOCK Nº1 |
| 49 | " Nº2 |
| 50 | " Nº3 |
| 51 | " Nº4 |
| 52 | " Nº5 |
| 53 | " Nº6 |
| 54 | " Nº7 |
| 55 | " Nº8 |
| 56 | " Nº9 |
| 57 | " Nº10 (PB70 ONLY) |
| 58 | " Nº11 |
| 59 | FWD COVERING BOARD SUPPORT |
| 60 | AFT COVERING BOARD SUPPORT |
| 61 | FWD COVERING BOARD SPACER |
| 62 | AFT COVERING BOARD SPACER (PB70 ONLY) |
| 63 | FWD. DECK |
| 64 | FWD. COVERING BOARD |
| 65 | AFT COVERING BOARD |
| 66 | SHEER MOULDING |
| 67A | FWD MONKEY RAIL |
| 67B | SIDE MONKEY RAIL |
| 67C | AFT MONKEY RAIL |

SHEET Nº4 — DWG Nº 63100

Fig. 4-21. Detail of deck framing.

line—sighting the sheer from a distance as you work. The details of the deck framing are shown in Fig. 4-21.

The framing for the cabin flooring should be installed now, but if you are planning to use an outboard motor instead of an inboard engine, it would be a good idea to cut the transom out for the correct height of the motor. This will make it easier to get in and out of the hull when you're cutting and fitting. If you're in doubt about the exact size of the motor you intend to use, you can obtain specifications by writing to the manufacturer. Whether you're going to use inboard or inboard-outboard drive, now is the time to get the framing in.

The construction details of the cabin floor are shown in Fig. 4-23 while the cabin top framing details are explained—by notes and drawings—in Fig. 4-24. As with the hull framing members, all the wooden members are already cut out for you and require only a light sanding before positioning and securing in place with glue and wood screws.

While framing the cabin, secure cleat stock #103 and #104 to the bulkhead and floor as indicated in Fig. 4-25. Keep these plumb and square when fitting into position. Apply glue and fasten with 1 1/4-inch screws on 6-inch centers. Maintain one-half inch extension of lavatory bulkhead when fastening in the cleat. Continue by

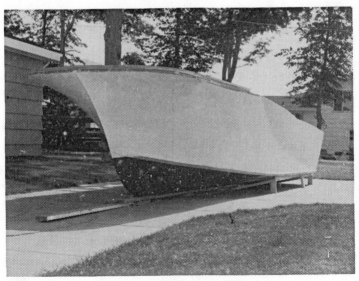

Fig. 4-22. Hull turned upright after applying planking.

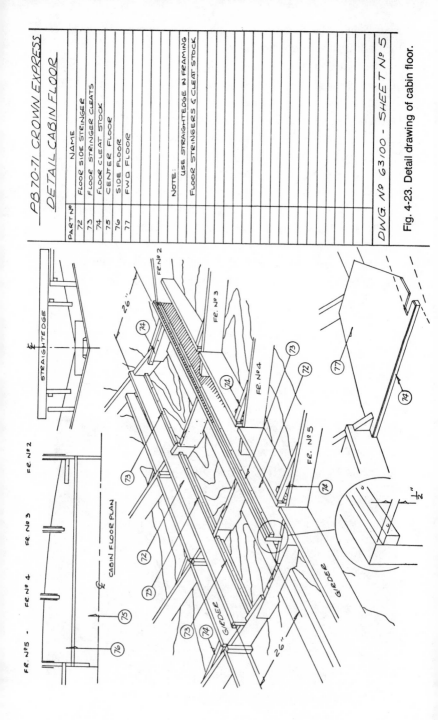

PB 70-71 CROWN EXPRESS

DETAIL CABIN FLOOR

| PART Nº | NAME |
|---|---|
| 72 | FLOOR SIDE STRINGER |
| 73 | FLOOR STRINGER CLEATS |
| 74 | FLOOR CLEAT STOCK |
| 75 | CENTER FLOOR |
| 76 | SIDE FLOOR |
| 77 | FWD FLOOR |

NOTE:
USE STRAIGHTEDGE IN FRAMING
FLOOR STRINGERS & CLEAT STOCK

DWG Nº 63100 - SHEET Nº 5

Fig. 4-23. Detail drawing of cabin floor.

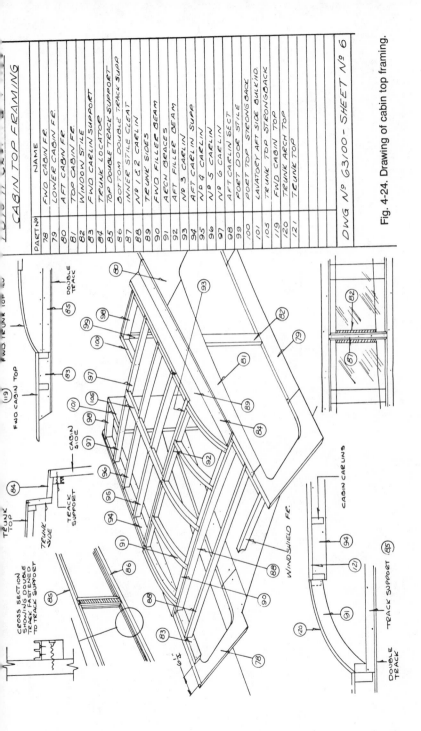

CABIN TOP FRAMING

| PART Nº | NAME |
|---|---|
| 78 | FWD CABIN FR. |
| 79 | LOWER CABIN FR. |
| 80 | AFT CABIN FR. |
| 81 | TOP CABIN FR. |
| 82 | WINDOW STILE |
| 83 | FWD CARLIN SUPPORT |
| 84 | TRUNK LOCATOR |
| 85 | TOP DOUBLE TRACK SUPPORT |
| 86 | BOTTOM DOUBLE TRACK SUPP |
| 87 | INNER STILE CLEAT |
| 88 | Nº 1 & 2 CARLIN |
| 89 | TRUNK SIDES |
| 90 | FWD FILLER BEAM |
| 91 | ARCH BRACES |
| 92 | AFT FILLER BEAM |
| 93 | Nº 3 CARLIN SUPP |
| 94 | AFT CARLIN SUPP |
| 95 | Nº 4 CARLIN |
| 96 | Nº 5 CARLIN |
| 97 | Nº 6 CARLIN |
| 98 | AFT CARLIN SECT |
| 99 | PORT DOOR STILE |
| 100 | PORT TOP STRONG BACK |
| 101 | LAVATORY AFT SIDE BULKHD. |
| 105 | TRUNK TOP STRONGBACK |
| 119 | FWD CABIN TOP |
| 120 | TRUNK ARCH TOP |
| 121 | TRUNK TOP |

DWG Nº 63/00 - SHEET Nº 6

Fig. 4-24. Drawing of cabin top framing.

95

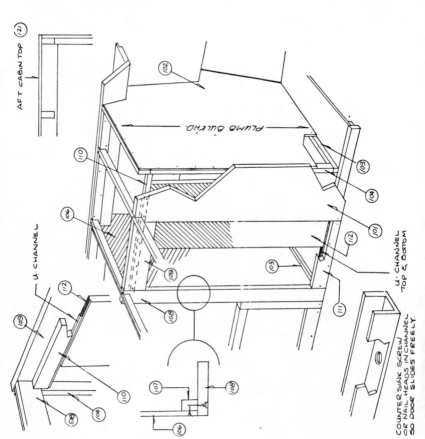

## PB70-71 CROWN EXPRESS
## LAVATORY DETAILS

| PART No | NAME |
|---------|------|
| 98 | AFT CARLIN SECT |
| 101 | LAVATORY AFT SIDE BULK'HD |
| 102 | AFT BULK'HD |
| 103 | BULK'HD. BOTTOM CLEAT STOCK |
| 104 | BULK'HD SIDE CLEAT STOCK |
| 106 | LAVATORY FWD BULK'HD. |
| 107 | LAV FWD INNER BULK'HD CLEAT |
| 108 | LAV FWD SIDE BULK'HD |
| 109 | LAV SIDE TOP BULK'HD |
| 110 | LAV TOP TRACK SUPP |
| 111 | LAV BOTTOM BULK'HD. |
| 112 | LAV DOOR |

DWG. N° 63/00 – SHEET N° 7

Fig. 4-25. Lavatory details.

96

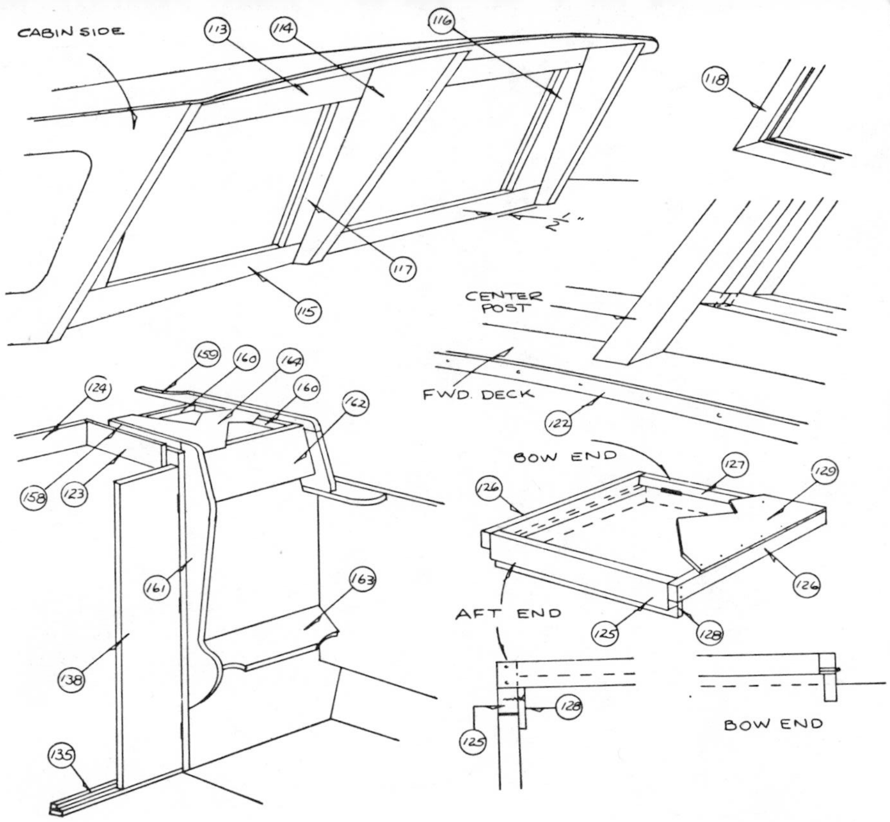

PB 70-71 CROWN EXPRESS

WINDSHIELD-DASH DETAIL

| PART Nº | NAME |
|---|---|
| 113 | WINDSHIELD TOP FR. |
| 114 | WINDSHIELD CENTER FR. |
| 115 | WINDSHIELD BOTTOM FR. |
| 116 | WINDSHIELD OUTER FR. |
| 117 | WINDSHIELD INNER FR. |
| 118 | WINDSHIELD FR. STOCK |
| 123 | HATCH SIDE CLEAT |
| 124 | HATCH FWD CLEAT |
| 125 | HATCH COVER AFT FR. |
| 126 | HATCH COVER SIDE FR. |
| 127 | HATCH COVER FWD FR. |
| 128 | HATCH DOOR STOP |
| 129 | HATCH TOP |
| 158 | DASH INNER CLEAT |
| 159 | DASH OUTER CLEAT |
| 160 | DASH FILLER |
| 161 | DASH LOWER TRIM |
| 162 | DASH |
| 163 | FOOT BOARD |
| 164 | TOP COVER |
| 135 | CABIN DOOR FLOOR CLEAT |
| 138 | CABIN DOOR |
| 122 | DECK BEAM CAP |

DWG. Nº 63100 — SHEET Nº 8

Fig. 4-26. Windshield-dash detail.

97

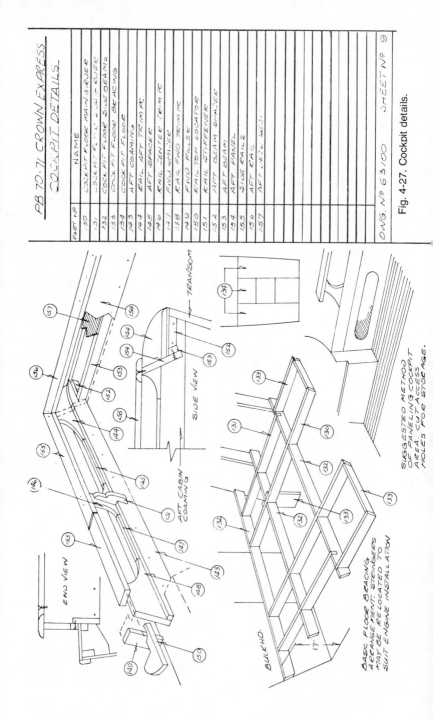

| PART No | NAME |
|---------|------|
| 130 | COCKPIT FLOOR MAIN GIRDER |
| 131 | COCKPIT FLOOR SIDE GIRDER |
| 132 | COCKPIT FLOOR SIDE BEAMS |
| 133 | COCKPIT FLOOR BEARING |
| 134 | COCKPIT FLOOR |
| 143 | AFT COAMING |
| 144 | RAIL AFT TRIM PC |
| 145 | AFT SPACER |
| 146 | RAIL CENTER TRIM PC |
| 147 | FWD WALKER |
| 148 | RAIL FWD TRIM PC |
| 149 | FWD FILLER |
| 150 | RAIL TOP LOCATOR |
| 151 | RAIL STIFFENER |
| 152 | AFT BEAM SPACER |
| 153 | AFT BEAM |
| 154 | AFT PANEL |
| 155 | SIDE RAILS |
| 156 | AFT RAIL |
| 157 | AFT DECK BEAM |

PB 70-71 CROWN EXPRESS
COCKPIT DETAILS

DWG. No 63100    SHEET No 9

Fig. 4-27. Cockpit details.

END VIEW

SIDE VIEW

TRANSOM

AFT CABIN COAMING

BULKHD.

17"

BASIC FLOOR BRACING ARRANGEMENT. STRINGERS MAY BE RELOCATED TO SUIT ENGINE INSTALLATION.

SUGGESTED METHOD OF PANELING COCKPIT AREA. CUT ACCESS HOLES FOR STORAGE.

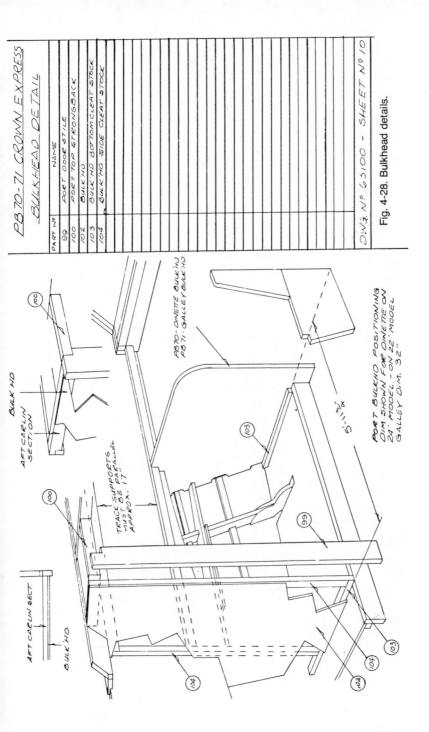

PB70-71 CROWN EXPRESS
BULKHEAD DETAIL

| PART Nº | NAME | | | | | | | | | | | | | | | | | | | | | | | | | |
|---|---|---|---|---|---|---|---|---|---|---|---|---|---|---|---|---|---|---|---|---|---|---|---|---|---|---|
| 99 | PORT DOOR STILE | | | | | | | | | | | | | | | | | | | | | | | | | |
| 100 | PORT TOP STRONGBACK | | | | | | | | | | | | | | | | | | | | | | | | | |
| 102 | BULKHD | | | | | | | | | | | | | | | | | | | | | | | | | |
| 103 | BULK'HD BOTTOM CLEAT STOCK | | | | | | | | | | | | | | | | | | | | | | | | | |
| 104 | BULK'HD SIDE CLEAT STOCK | | | | | | | | | | | | | | | | | | | | | | | | | |

DWG. Nº 63100 - SHEET Nº 10

Fig. 4-28. Bulkhead details.

BULK HD

AFT CARLIN SECTION

AFT CARLIN SECT.

BULK HD

TRACK SUPPORTS MUST BE PARALLEL APPROX. 17"

PB70 - DINETTE BULKHD
PB71: GALLEY BULKHD

5'-11 7/16"

PORT BULKHD POSITIONING DIM SHOWN FOR DINETTE ON 24' MODEL - ON 22' MODEL GALLEY DIM. 32"

99

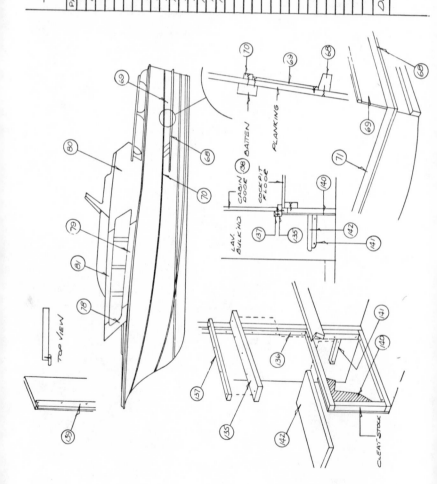

| PART Nº | NAME |
|---|---|
| 68 | FENDER RAIL |
| 69 | TRIM PANEL |
| 70 | HULL RAILS |
| 71 | AFT FENDER RAIL |
| 78 | FWD CABIN FR |
| 79 | LOWER CABIN FR |
| 80 | AFT CABIN FR |
| 81 | TOP CABIN FR |
| 135 | CABIN DOOR FLOOR CLEAT |
| 136 | CABIN DOOR SIDE STOPS |
| 137 | CABIN DOOR BOTTOM STOP |
| 138 | CABIN DOOR SECTION |
| 139 | CABIN DOOR FLANGE |
| 140 | RISER PANEL |
| 141 | STEP CLEAT |
| 142 | STEP |

PB 70-71 CROWN CRUISER
CABIN DETAILS

DWG Nº 63100 - SHEET Nº 11

Fig. 4-29. Cabin details.

100

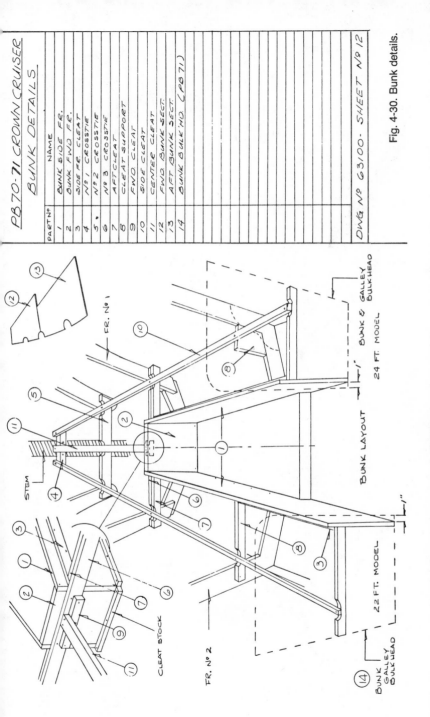

| PART N° | NAME |
|---|---|
| 1 | BUNK SIDE FR. |
| 2 | BUNK FWD FR. |
| 3 | SIDE FR. CLEAT |
| 4 | N°1 CROSSTIE |
| 5 | N°2 CROSSTIE |
| 6 | N°3 CROSSTIE |
| 7 | AFT CLEAT |
| 8 | CLEAT SUPPORT |
| 9 | FWD CLEAT |
| 10 | SIDE CLEAT |
| 11 | CENTER CLEAT |
| 12 | FWD BUNK SECT. |
| 13 | AFT BUNK SECT. |
| 14 | BUNK BULK'HD (PB 71) |

PB70-71 CROWN CRUISER
BUNK DETAILS

DWG N° G3100- SHEET N°12

Fig. 4-30. Bunk details.

101

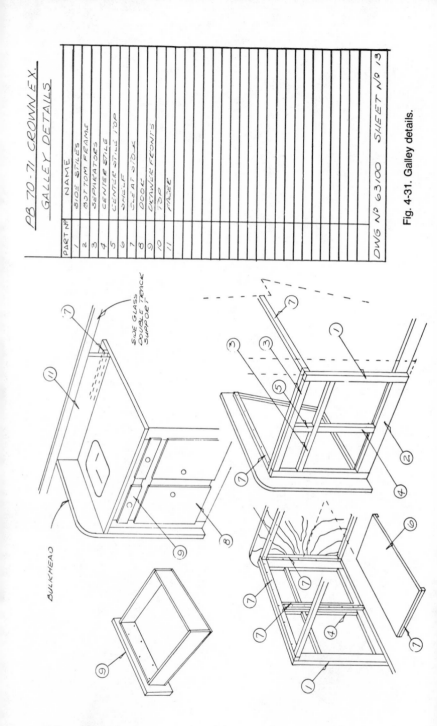

Fig. 4-31. Galley details.

PB 70-71 CROWN EX.
GALLEY DETAILS

| PART Nº | NAME |
|---------|------|
| 1 | SIDE STILES |
| 2 | BOTTOM FRAME |
| 3 | SEPARATORS |
| 4 | CENTER STILE |
| 5 | CENTER STILE TOP |
| 6 | SHELF |
| 7 | CLEAT STOCK |
| 8 | DOOR |
| 9 | DRAWER FRONTS |
| 10 | TOP |
| 11 | FACE |

DWG Nº 63100    SHEET Nº 13

SIDE GLASS
DOUBLE TRACK
SUPPORT

BULKHEAD

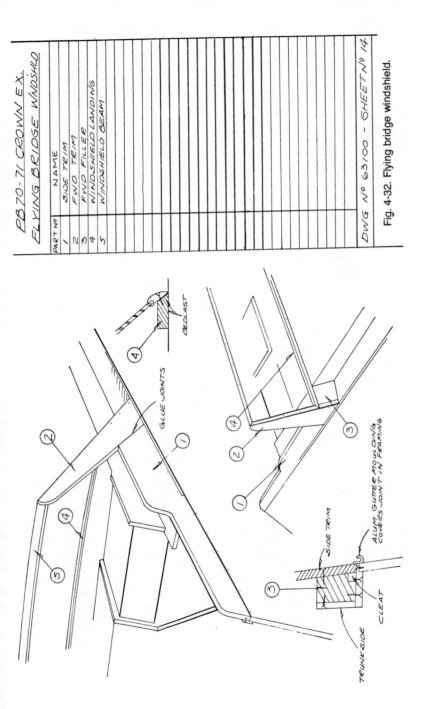

PB 70-71 CROWN EX.
ELYING BRIDGE WINDSHLD.

| PART Nº | NAME |
|---------|------|
| 1 | SIDE TRIM |
| 2 | FWD TRIM |
| 3 | FWD FILLER |
| 4 | WINDSHIELD LANDING |
| 5 | WINDSHIELD BEAM |

DWG Nº 63/00 - SHEET Nº 14

Fig. 4-32. Flying bridge windshield.

GLUE JOINTS

BEDLAST

SIDE TRIM

ALUM. GUTTER MOULDING
COVERS JOINT IN FRAMING

CLEAT

TRUNK-SIDE

103

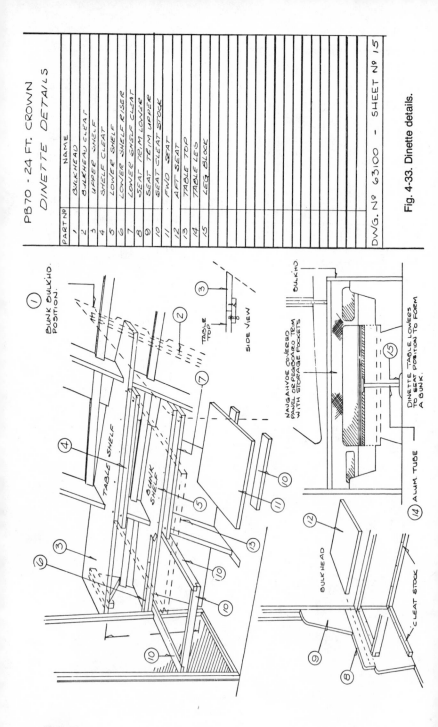

PB70 - 24 FT. CROWN
DINETTE DETAILS

| PART N° | NAME |
|---|---|
| 1 | BULKHEAD |
| 2 | BULKHEAD CLEAT |
| 3 | UPPER SHELF |
| 4 | SHELF CLEAT |
| 5 | LOWER SHELF |
| 6 | LOWER SHELF RISER |
| 7 | LOWER SHELF CLEAT |
| 8 | SEAT TRIM LOWER |
| 9 | SEAT TRIM UPPER |
| 10 | SEAT CLEAT STOCK |
| 11 | FWD SEAT |
| 12 | AFT SEAT |
| 13 | TABLE TOP |
| 14 | TABLE LEG |
| 15 | LEG BLOCK |

DWG. N° 63100 - SHEET N° 15

Fig. 4-33. Dinette details.

104

fitting and fastening the aft bulkhead and then the forward lavatory bulkhead. Take you time and trim just enough for a tight fit at the joints for a neater appearance.

Windshield-dash details are shown in Fig. 4-26, cockpit details in Fig. 4-27, bulkhead details in Fig. 4-28, cabin details in Fig. 4-29, and the bunk details in Fig. 4-30. When these steps are completed, follow normal finishing and painting procedures. This is one of the most important phases in producing a good looking and professional job. Upon completion of this phase, continue on the galley and dinette installations as well as the finishing of the cabin interior.

When installing the galley framing (Fig. 4-31), use a framing square to check that all door openings are square and plumb. Install side stile #1 by butting it to lavatory bulkhead at the side and to the floor stringer at the bottom. Glue all framing in position and secure with wood screws as called for in the instructions. Simple drawers and cabinet doors may be made up from plywood scraps which can then be rabbetted if desired. Mount the splash board and cleat flush with the cabin side and install doors using standard cupboard hinges, knobs and catches. The construction details of the galley are shown in Fig. 4-33, and if you want to add the flying bridge windshield, consult Fig. 4-32 for details.

When a project like this one is completed, you will have graduated from the amateur field and jumped—very quickly—into the professional arena. Moreover, you will own a boat that can be used by the whole family for fishing, week-end cruises, and the like. Best of all, you will have a $14,000 cruiser of which you can be proud and it cost you only about half the amount—depending upon the accessories you added. To learn where you can find more details about these accessories and about motors, refer to the listings in Chapter 3.

# Building Boats from Purchased Plans

One of the main reasons for building your own boat is to save as much money as possible. Some amateurs begin with one of the various kits on the market, and while these kits do save the builder time and money, many of the items in these kits are merely "stock" items—available anywhere. If these same items are purchased locally by the builder, they are cheaper (and more convenient) than if the kit dealer purchases, fabricates, and then distributes them. Therefore, you can build your boat cheaper by purchasing a set of plans (already tested) and full size patterns. Then purchase your materials locally where they're least expensive.

Anyone with average do-it-yourself abilities and who can follow directions can build his or her boat from purchased plans. Even the more complicated designs are within the capability of the average handyman. Naturally, on the large designs—like sloops and cruisers over 15 feet—it is recommended that the builder have some past experience constructing a smaller boat.

How much money you save by building from plans and materials purchased locally depends on a large number of variables. Materials and equipment all vary in cost depending on quality or type used. However, most builders will tell you that they have saved from 30% to 50% of the cost of a comparable factory-built boat. Those persons who are adept at scrounging for the best buys in lumber and materials can save even more.

If the plans are purchased from reputable firms and designers, you can be certain that much research and testing has gone into the design to insure that your finished boat will look and perform right. However, all boat plans on the market are not alike. For example, some of the plans offered for sale are very well designed, but since they include little or no step-by-step instructions, they aren't complete enough for the amateur's purposes. Still other plans appear to have been designed by armchair dreamers and not naval architects.

When selecting a set of plans and instructions for the type of boat you want, keep the following in mind: Choose a design that has been proven—actually built and tested; large scale plans should be available for certain complicated parts of the boat; plans should include a list of materials and a fastening schedule when wood construction is involved; written as well as pictorial instructions should be provided; buy your plans from firms which will answer the amateur's questions promptly and expertly. Look beyond mere plans "brokers"; insist upon boat designers.

The designs offered by dealers in boat plans range from paddleboards and dinghies (Fig. 5-1) through ski cruisers (Fig. 5-2) to ocean-going cruising yachts (Fig. 5-3). Most of these designs can be built with ordinary hand tools as described in Chapter 2, but, naturally, the more tools you have, the easier the job will be. For example, on the larger designs, a circular saw as well as a band saw is desirable. However, none of the designs will require equipment that the average builder can't operate. Special items, like large wood clamps, can usually be borrowed or rented for the brief period you will need them.

If you can find the exact design to suit your desires, then all is well; if not, many of the plans purchased from dealers can be modified somewhat. In fact, adding features to your boat is one of the joys of building your own craft. However, stay away from modifications that would impair the balance or performance of the craft—you don't want a monstrosity. In general, the boat length may be increased or decreased up to about 10% on most designs. (Sailboats are an exception.) Modifications in length may be carried out by replacing the frames (forms) a proportional amount while you're

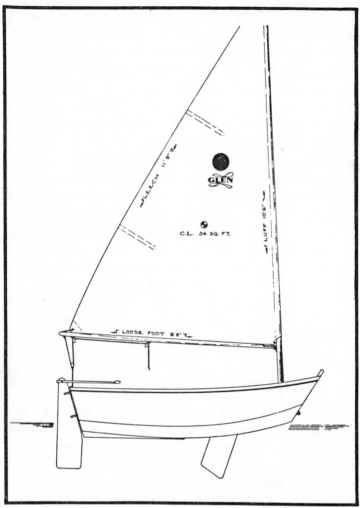

Fig. 5-1. An 8-foot sailing dinghy that is easily and quickly constructed by the beginning boatbuilder.

building. Before jumping into such a project, however, always check with the firm supplying the plans to make sure the change is acceptable.

## PLYWOOD BOATS

For the majority of amateur boatbuilders, plywood construction will offer the easiest and least expensive method of building. Written and pictorial instructions accompanying plywood plans are usually geared to the abilities of the amateur, but will generate a boat with the appearance and performance of a professional product. An example of the typical procedures used to build a plywood boat from purchased plans and locally-bought materials follows:

Many of the smaller designs do not require any kind of building form; the hulls are merely built upside down for ease of construction. The hulls of the larger designs, however, are normally erected on a simple building form constructed of scrap lumber.

Framing members determine the shape of the hull and can be cut out and assembled by using full size patterns accompanying the plans. After assembly the framing members are transferred to the building form.

The next step is to secure the framing members. This is done by springing longitudinal members (common stock available at the local lumber yard) between each framing member. The longitudinal members should fit snugly in notches; this makes for a rigid, sturdy boat structure. In the better designs available to the amateur boatbuilder, no steam bending of the longitudinal members is required.

Once in place, all members are faired or beveled so that the sheet plywood planking will mate flat at all contact areas. Usually a box plane is the only tool necessary.

The plywood panels used with most boat plans are cut oversize. The builder usually finds that gluing and fastening them is a quick and easy operation. The framework soon assumes a "pattern" which the builder uses as a guide to the contour of the planking panels. Overhanging edges are trimmed off flush with the framing members.

After the planking is applied, the boat hull is turned over. It'll remain in this position for the balance of construction. The final phase of construction will involve the installation of decking, seats, etc.

Priming and painting the entire boat and then installing hardware (if any) just about finishes the project. Using plywood for boat construction puts boatbuilding within the reach of nearly everyone.

## TYPES OF DESIGNS AVAILABLE

The array of boat designs available in plan form would fill a large book—even a set of volumes; but let's just look at a sampling of some of the designs suitable for the amateur boatbuilder.

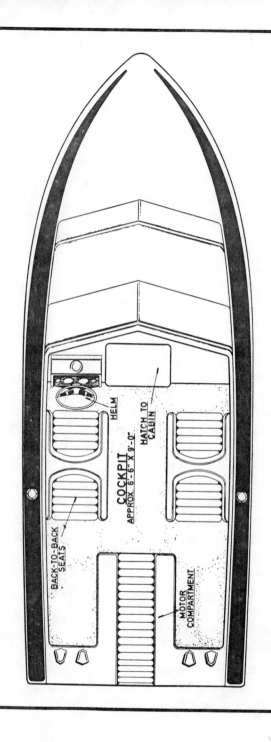

HELM

HATCH TO CABIN

COCKPIT
APPROX. 6'-6" X 9'-0"

BACK-TO-BACK
SEATS

MOTOR COMPARTMENT

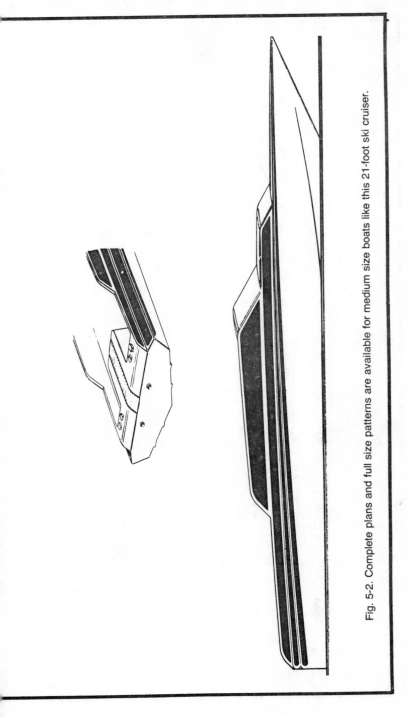

Fig. 5-2. Complete plans and full size patterns are available for medium size boats like this 21-foot ski cruiser.

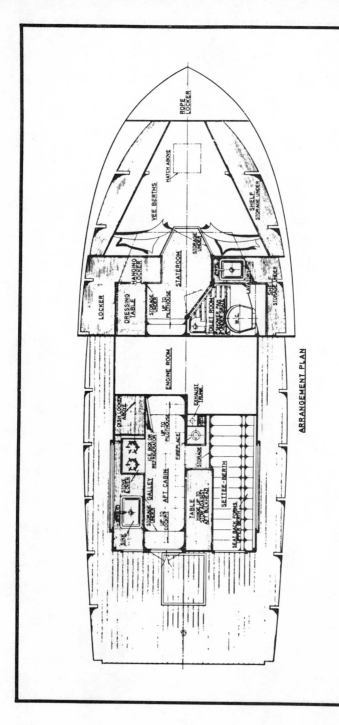

ARRANGEMENT PLAN

ROPE LOCKER

VEE BERTHS

HATCH ABOVE

SHELF
STORAGE UNDER

STATEROOM

HANGING LOCKER

STORAGE UNDER

LOCKER

DRESSING TABLE

STORAGE UP TO PILOTHOUSE

LAVATORY

TOILET ROOM
SHOWER PAN
SHOWER DRAIN

SHELF
STORAGE UNDER

W.C.

ENGINE ROOM

EXHAUST TRUNK

DISH LOCKER ABOVE

ICE BOX OR REFRIGERATOR

UP TO PILOTHOUSE

FIREPLACE

STOVE LOCKER

GALLEY

AFT CABIN

STORAGE UNDER

UP TO LOCKER

STORAGE

SETTEE-BERTH

SINK

TABLE
HINGE UP. AFT BULKHEAD

SEAT BACK FORMS UPPER BERTH

112

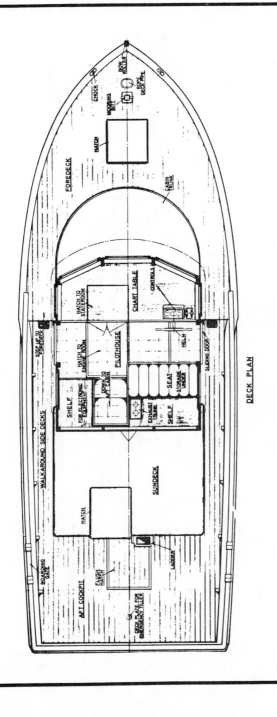

DECK PLAN

Fig. 5-3. While not for the beginner, you can purchase plans, full size patterns, and complete instructions to build this 28-foot cruising yacht and sail away to a tropical island. (Continued on next page.)

113

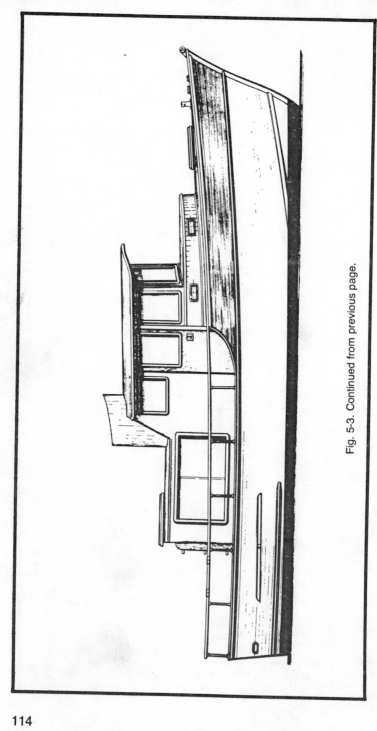

Fig. 5-3. Continued from previous page.

114

How about a 10-foot flat bottom rowboat like the one in Fig. 5-4? Complete plans plus full size patterns for the stem, transom, knee, seat brace, and building forms for this boat are available from Glen L Marine Designs, 9152 Rosecrans, Bellflower, Calif. 90706 for less than $10. This small craft is not only excellent for fishing in protected waters, but can be used for many other purposes. For example, this boat can be stowed easily aboard a larger cruiser and used as a ship-to-shore dinghy. Its light weight makes it suitable for transporting either in the back of a pickup or on top of a car. It can then easily be carried to the water by two men. It is easy to row, pole, or paddle, but an outboard motor up to 5 HP can also be used.

This versatile little boat is not only a practical size for many uses, but is inexpensive to build. To illustrate, the planking (for the sides and bottom) consists of conventional 4' × 8' sheets of exterior plywood and you can plank the whole boat with two and a half sheets and have material left over. The simply constructed hull is built bottom side up over building forms that are later discarded. The straightforward construction should enable the average handyman to build the hull on a weekend at a greatest cost of well under $100.

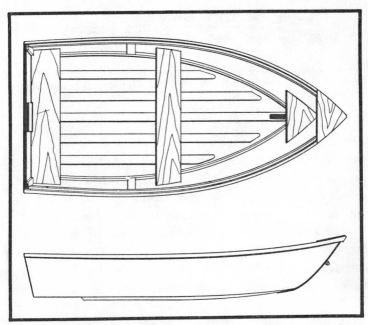

Fig. 5-4. An easily constructed 10-foot flat bottom rowboat available in plan form.

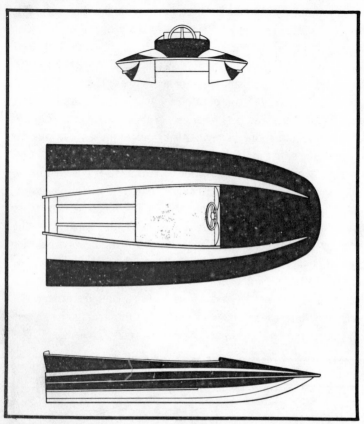

Fig. 5-5. If you're one who fancies high speed, then this 10-foot tunnel-hull racing boat might be for you.

If you're one who fancies high speed races, then the 10-foot tunnel hull racing boat shown in Fig. 5-5 just might be the one for you. The air cushion effect between the twin hulls on this design makes for a smoother ride and, by reducing resistance, makes high speeds possible with low horsepower motors.

Since its beam is less than 5 feet and its hull weighs less than 120 pounds, this boat is suitable for transporting in the family wagon, on a car roof, or in the back of a pickup. The design of this craft—although the rakish appearance enhances the illusion of speed—is entirely safe for protected waters when powered as recommended by the designers.

Construction of this craft is simple and direct when the plans, full size patterns, and instructions are followed. Again, a Glen L design comes with a full list of materials and a fastening schedule. If you want to rush the construction of this boat a bit, a frame kit is available for less than $100.

The 14-foot sloop shown in Fig. 5-6 is designed for sporty sailing and it is one that the whole family can enjoy. With her generous sail area she's a lively boat even in the lightest breezes and her rig permits easy handling with a minimum crew. The broad beam not only makes this craft safe and stable, but allows plenty of room in

Fig. 5-6. This 14-foot sloop designed for sporty sailing is one the whole family can enjoy.

the cockpit for the whole family plus a couple of friends. If you desire to use auxiliary power, a small outboard motor (3 to 5 HP) may be mounted. Then you can leave the sails in the bag and use the vessel for a fishing skiff or utility boat when the need arises.

This craft—called the Glen L 14—is an easy boat to build, even for the amateur. All details necessary for construction from plywood are clearly given in the large scale drawings, step-by-step instructions, or the full sized patterns which eliminate the lofting process. A complete set of plans with full sized patterns for the centerboard, centerboard trunk, stem, rudder, breasthook, and half section templates for the frames and transom may be purchased for less than $20. To simplify the building process, you can purchase a frame kit for about $125.

The lightweight plywood construction keeps the costs low and makes trailering and launching a simple process. You can completely outfit this craft from the items contained in the following kits.

> Hardware Kit includes: rudder gudgeons and pintles, rudder stop, gooseneck, all jam cleats, mast tangs, chainplates with covers, mast-head sheave with pin, eye strip, bow plate, jib halyard block, mainsheet blocks, shackles, swivel eye blocks on plates, adjustable jib sheet slides on tracks with stops, centerboard sheave, centerboard pulley, and centerboard weight.
>
> Rigging Kit includes: all stainless steel shrouds and forestay with swages fittings and forestay turn-buckle, shroud adjusters, all halyards, centerboard lift, and all sheets of "yacht braid" line.
>
> Sails: both main and jib, made from Dacron with matching sail bag.
>
> Spar Kit: aluminum mast, masthead fitting with sheaves, hound fitting, mast tangs, gooseneck, end cap, jib halyard block with fittings, and all required jam cleats.

To secure more information about this craft, write Glen L Marine Designs, 9152 Rosecrans, Bellflower, Calif. 90706.

The big luxury runabouts like the one shown in Fig. 5-7 have been smash successes at all the recent boat shows, but until recently, the prices of these boats have been too much for all but the most affluent. Now by purchasing detailed plans (with step-by-step instructions) and procuring materials locally, the amateur boatbuilder can have his own luxury runabout for a fraction of the boat show cost.

The boat in Fig. 5-7, called Bolero by its designers, has all the specifications of a high performance rough water runabout. The hull is 24 1/2 feet long and just under 8 feet wide (legal for trailering).

Ken Hankinson, the designer at Glen L Marine, created a 20-degree deep vee hull for the Bolero. Lift strakes are positioned at critical points in the hull. The bottom is composed of two thicknesses of plywood sheeting laid diagonal to the craft's long axis. Special features are the soft entry bulbous keel and a reverse curve at the chine to ensure a dry ride.

The most notable feature of the Bolero—according to its designers—is its ability to carry power—lots of power. The boat can handle single or twin motors using outdrive or vee drive transmis-

Fig. 5-7. This big luxury runabout is within reach of the amateur boatbuilder when complete plans and step-by-step instructions are followed.

sions. Either gasoline or diesel fuel is suitable and its 90 to 120 gallon fuel capacity makes for long hours of operating without refueling. Maximum weight of an outdrive unit is 1200 pounds, while the vee drive motors can run to 1600 pounds.

The Bolero has plush accommodations for fun on any protected water. The sundeck aft is a large area measuring 75″ × 54″. In keeping with the high performance concept, the self-draining cockpit has an L-shaped lounge seat plus a control station. For those who go in for overnight cruising (or a daytime nap, for that matter), there is a cuddy cabin with berths for two.

The plans for this craft include full size patterns for all the hull framing members; this makes lofting unnecessary. Complete procedural and pictorial instructions allow the builder to complete the job in a smooth manner. All this costs less than $50. If you want to hurry the job along, a complete frame kit is available for around $400.

The construction of this boat is certainly not what one would call simple. Yet, with its comprehensive instructions, this project is not out of the reach of the amateur boatbuilder—especially if he already has a smaller building project under his belt. The total cost will vary considerably—depending upon many variables—but the complete cost of the hull (less motors) should run less than $1500.

The plan and elevation views of another rapid rig are shown in Fig. 5-8. This 17-foot ski boat, when equipped with the right power,

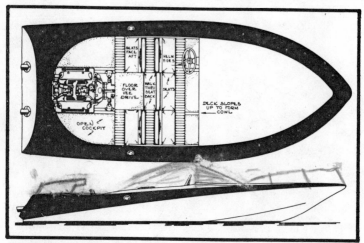

Fig. 5-8. Plan and elevation views of another rapid rig for which plans and complete instructions are available.

will get up and "GO." You can use this craft for dragging, ski towing, or just plain old getting out and going—as fast as you want to.

The appearance of this craft—called Thunderbolt—is impressive, as you can readily see in the photograph (Fig. 5-9). The transom in itself is very unusual, but the plans give you the option of mounting a vertical member if you prefer. All of the necessary details of contruction are provided for the building of this rig, including step-by-step photos of an actual project. The motor is installed at the stern of the boat and must be connected to a vee drive to maintain the proper hull balance. The motor in a boat of this type is usually left exposed and a goodly amount of chrome plate and paint is normally used to enhance its appearance.

The fast and positive way to build your own rapid rig is to use a frame kit which contains: frames fully assembled, transom fully framed, stem, and breasthook. This entire package, complete with plans, bill of materials, and fastening schedule can be purchased for less than $200. On this model, you can also buy a fiberglass covering kit as well as a fastening kit for increasing the rig's rigidity.

## FIBERGLASS BOAT DESIGNS

Any plywood boat may be fiberglassed to some extent. Perhaps you'll only want to use fiberglass tape (of various widths) to ensure tight seams on your craft. Maybe you will fiberglass the bottom or even the whole hull of your boat with fiberglass cloth. For projects of this sort, Chapter 9 gives all the basic details including step-by-step instructions for many boat maintenance and repair situations using fiberglass.

Although fiberglass boats have been on the market for quite some time, the construction of an entire boat has been impractical for the amateur boatbuilder because of the costly molds required. However, two processes developed over a period of years have now been refined to the point where it is not only possible, but also practical, for the home boatbuilder to use this revolutionary material. Now you can enjoy the many benefits inherent in stock fiberglass boats and save money by doing the job yourself. It is also possible to equal or surpass the quality of factory-built fiberglass boats because *you* can control the quality. The price of building a fiberglass boat is only slightly more than the price of building a

Fig. 5-9. The boat in Fig. 5-8 after completion.

comparable plywood boat, and the techniques are well within the abilities of the average handyman—even one who has never built a boat before.

Most factory-built fiberglass hulls are formed inside female molds. These molds are especially adapted to assembly line techniques and are very expensive...so much so that in most cases you could purchase a new factory-built boat for less than the cost of the mold. Obviously, many boats must be made and sold from one mold to justify the expense of producing it. Molds are definitely not for the amateur builder who only wants to build one hull. However, he can still construct his own fiberglass hull by following either of two practical procedures: the fiberglass planking method or the PVC (plastic) foam sandwich core method. The essential difference between these methods and the factory method is the gender of the mold: the factory uses a female mold and the amateur a male mold.

Here's how the fiberglass planking method works. The male mold is constructed similar to the way the frame of a regular plywood boat is constructed; that is, the transom, frames, stem, breasthook, etc., are assembled and secured (bottom up). Suitable lengths of fiberglass planking are cut from a roll, laid around the hull and fastened in place. The fiberglass material conforms readily to any contour. Fiberglass laminate is then built up over the resin coated fiberglass planking and is allowed time to form a stiff strong hull before the entire hull is sanded and finished. The hull is then removed from the form and turned upright so that the interior of the boat can be completed.

The PVC foam sandwich core is also formed over a male mold but the structure of the mold differs: the frames are more widely spaced and closely spaced longitudinal battens—built from ordinary lumber—are secured across the frames. In place of planking, sheets of easily shaped PVC foam material are fastened to the mold. Fiberglass laminate is then built up over the form. The hull is then sanded and finished, removed from the form, and supported right side up in cradles. Again fiberglass laminate is applied to the inside of the hull and finished. The resulting boat is amazingly stiff, strong, and lightweight.

The foam sandwich material is somewhat more costly than the fiberglass planking material, but the foam hull has especially strong resistance to impact damage. The foam confers greater buoyancy than the planking and its heat and sound insulative qualities make for a quieter hull free of condensate on the interior surfaces. The fiberglass planking, however, does not require quite as elaborate a mold as the foam sandwich, and it is somewhat easier to build. Both materials give excellent results when the boat is designed and built properly.

Since more people are familiar with woodworking than with fiberglass, most amateur boatbuilders at first will find it easier to work with plywood when constructing their own vessel. However, once these same amateurs learn the techniques required by fiberglass—although it'll take some time—most of them will prefer to work with it.

Actually, working with fiberglass is not beyond the capabilities of the amateur boatbuilder; but fiberglass *is* messy and it *does* require special handling. If you have any doubts about your ability to do the job, talk to someone who has worked with fiberglass, or else try it on a small inexpensive craft to see how you like the material before attempting a larger vessel. In this way you will have a minimal investment (should you goof), and if you like the process, this first project can serve as a ship-to-shore dinghy for your larger boat, or you can even sell it (most likely for a nice profit).

If you're new at this game, the question is certain to come up...why fiberglass? This is not an easy question to answer and opinions will vary from builder to builder, but most people will agree that fiberglass hulls are easier to maintain, have a neater appearance, and are more leak-proof than plywood boats. Of course, a plywood boat can be fiberglassed to gain these advantages, but then you will have a heavier boat.

Don't worry about any special tools or equipment, because the same hand and portable power tools that are used for building plywood boats are all that are usually required. The only possible addition would be a good quality heavy duty disc sander. If you don't have one of these and don't wish to purchase one, you should know that they can usually be rented from a local hardware store or builder's supply house. Otherwise, no tools or equipment that the average handyman can't handle are necessary, and anyone can master the disc sander in very little time.

A recommended project for the beginner is an 11-foot fiberglass sloop like the one shown in Fig. 5-10. Plan and elevation drawings of this boat are shown in Fig. 5-11. This sloop-rigged sailboat is designed specifically for the fiberglass planking material described earlier. This material, used with a simple male mold, will enable the

Fig. 5-10. A recommended fiberglass project for the beginner is this 11-foot sloop.

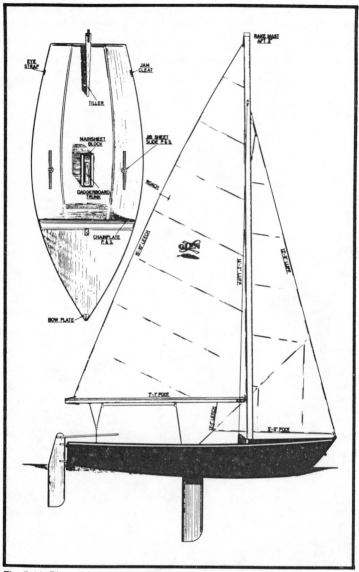

Fig. 5-11. Plan and elevation views of the craft in Fig. 5-10.

amateur to build a fiberglass hull that is equal or superior to the factory-built, female-mold hulls.

The designers, Glen L Marine Designs, claim that this boat is extremely responsive—offering exhilarating performance. With its lightweight hull and generous sloop rig, the craft points high, answers the helm quickly, moves along well in light airs as well as strong breezes, and is extremely well balanced. The boat has the feel and speed of a much larger boat, and yet the compact size allows the boat to be car-topped, carried in a pickup, or stowed inside most station wagons with relative ease. Best of all, the air chambers along the hull sides and below the foredeck make the craft unsinkable.

The plans for this sloop include full size patterns for form members, daggerboard, daggerboard case, and rudder. Also included are step-by-step instructions (with numerous photographs) for construction. Nothing is left to chance.

A form frame kit makes fabricating this boat a pleasure. The kit resembles conventional frame kits except that exterior plywood and non-marine wood is specified for the members (since most of the members are merely used to establish the correct shape of the hull and don't remain aboard the completed boat). The form frame kit contains: transom form, 10 athwartship forms and bulkheads, and the stem form. Also included are the rudder, tiller, daggerboard, and daggerboard cap; all are machine-shaped from solid mahogany and ready for finishing.

Sails, spar kits, hardware kits, rigging kits, and other fiberglassing supplies can be obtained from Glen L Marine Designs, 9152 Rosecrans, Bellflower, Calif. 90706.

# Build an Eskimo Boat for Practically Nothing

When most people hear the word "kayak," their thoughts turn to the Eskimo of the Far North...paddling his long and narrow whalebone and walrus-hide craft through perilous ice floes. And no wonder. It is known far and wide that the Eskimo's very survival depends on this fragile, skin-over-framework vessel.

The walrus (or bearded seal) skin on the early kayak models covered the bottom and all of the deck area except for a small round opening (the cockpit) at the craft's center. After taking his seat in the cockpit, the Eskimo would button to his waist a skin apron fastened to the deck surrounding the opening. Thus, the craft was made watertight. With such an arrangement, the Eskimo could propel his boat with a double-ended paddle in the roughest waters without fear of being swamped. The boat could capsize, roll over and come upright (with the aid of the boatman's paddle) without shipping water. In stormy waters the kayak was sometimes intentionally capsized to avoid a heavy wave. The kayak would be rolled upright after the wave had passed. The entire procedure took only a few seconds.

The Eskimo used his kayak for hunting hair seals in open water. To most of us, however, a kayak is for venturing. Whisk along the edge of a fast-moving stream or shoot the rapids...ease along the shore of a river or lake in search of lunker bass or explore hidden coves and tributaries...creep out on a marsh in the frosty early morning to wait for the first pass of mallards. This is just a sampling of a kayak's many uses.

Since driftwood, whalebone, and seal and walrus skins are rather difficult to come by these days, you'll probably want to substitute oak, mahogany or spruce for the whalebone and perhaps Douglas fir for the walrus skin. In fact, the craft described in this chapter is especially designed for the use of these woods.

You'll like the simple construction of this tough little lightweight that can be carried without much effort almost anywhere. Its 65-pound hull can even be car topped by one person if necessary. Three sheets of plywood will suffice for all planking—making this kayak not only easy to build, but inexpensive as well.

Unlike most of the kayak designs available to the amateur boatbuilder, this one does not have a flat bottom. Rather, it incorporates a round bottom (just like the Eskimo kayaks) and double ends—characteristics which enable the craft to move smoothly and easily through almost any kind of protected water.

There's no tricky toolwork either. The hull can be assembled without a jig; all you'll need are a few of the hand tools described in Chapter 2, the materials in the list to follow, and about 60 manhours (if this is your first project). If you already have one or two craft under your belt, then the time can be cut almost in half.

All of the materials required to build this boat should be on hand at your local lumber or building supplies dealer. When purchasing materials, make certain that all lumber is free from shakes and knots. When you have the option, choose the material of lightest weight. Of course, any lumber with qualities similar to the kind listed may be substituted; but again, try to get the lightest lumber that can do the job.

Because it is finished extensively, a board listed as 1 inch by the lumberyard actually will measure 3/4 inch. Boards listed as 2 inches will measure 1 5/8 inches. Therefore, stock for the frames and stems will be slightly narrower than the nominal widths. All other widths mentioned in this text or shown on the drawings are *net*—the exact size indicated.

The plywood panels for this craft (and all other boats for that matter) must be of an exterior or waterproof type. Although longer lengths of plywood may be used, the layout description is for standard 4′ × 8′ panels with the faces designated as A or B or better. Douglas fir plywood is considered satisfactory in all cases.

Screws and other fastenings throughout should be hot dipped galvanized or bronze. All joints should be glued with a hard setting waterproof glue, plastic resin, or resorcinol. Certain types of adhesives, however, are incompatible with oak and some other species, so check the manufacturer's data carefully before applying.

We suggest that the builder read through the entire text and review the drawings carefully before starting construction. Enlarged plans and full size frame patterns are available from Glen L Marine Designs, 9152 E. Rosecrans, Bellflower, Calif.

### LIST OF MATERIALS

| Item | Material | No. Pcs. | Size |
|---|---|---|---|
| Knees #2, Frames #3 | Oak, mahog., spruce | 1 | 1″ × 8″ × 7′6″ |
| Stem #1 | Douglas fir | 1 | 2″ × 6″ × 5′0″ |
| Keel | Oak, mahog., spruce | 1 | 1″ × 3″ × 8′4″ |
| Strongback | Oak, mahog., spruce | 1 | 1″ × 2″ × 12′0″ |
| Chine | Oak, mahog., spruce | 2 | 1″ × 1 1/4″ × 12′0″ |
| Sheer | Oak, mahog., spruce | 2 | 1″ × 1″ × 12′0″ |
| Skeg | Oak, mahog., spruce | 1 | 1″ × 1″ × 8′0″ |
| Planking | D.F. ext. plywood AB | 2 | 4′ × 8′ × 3/16″ or 1/4″ |
| Decking | D.F. ext. plywood AB | 1 | 4′ × 8′ × 1/8″ |
| Blocking | Scrap from frames | | 1″ (thickness) |

**Fastenings:** Bronze or hot dipped galvanized.

    Nails—Annular type boat nails
        3/4″ #14 - 1lb.

    Screws—Flat head, slotted, wood type.
        3/4″ #8 - 3 gross
        1″ #8 - 6 doz.
        1 1/2″ #8 - 8 doz.

    Glue—5 lbs. or 1 gal. of plastic resin or resorcinol type.

    Paint—1 qt. wood primer
        1 qt. boat enamel (color of your choice)

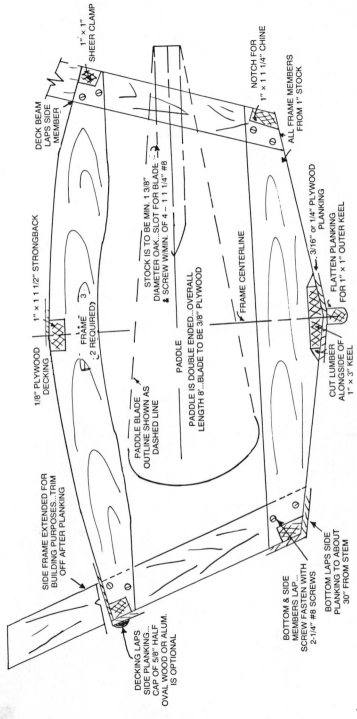

Fig. 6-1. Construction details of the two wooden frames.

1" × 1" SHEER CLAMP

DECK BEAM LAPS SIDE MEMBER

NOTCH FOR 1" × 1 1/4" CHINE

ALL FRAME MEMBERS FROM 1" STOCK

STOCK IS TO BE MIN. 1 3/8" DIAMETER OAK...SLOT FOR BLADE & SCREW W/MIN. OF 4 – 1 1 1/4" #8

1" × 1 1/2" STRONGBACK

1/8" PLYWOOD DECKING

FRAME (2 REQUIRED)

PADDLE

FRAME CENTERLINE

PADDLE BLADE OUTLINE SHOWN AS DASHED LINE

PADDLE IS DOUBLE ENDED...OVERALL LENGTH 8'...BLADE TO BE 3/8" PLYWOOD

3/16" or 1/4" PLYWOOD PLANKING

FLATTEN PLANKING FOR 1" × 1" OUTER KEEL

CUT LUMBER ALONGSIDE OF 1" × 3" KEEL

SIDE FRAME EXTENDED FOR BUILDING PURPOSES...TRIM OFF AFTER PLANKING

DECKING LAPS SIDE PLANKING... CAP OF 5/8" HALF OVAL WOOD OR ALUM. IS OPTIONAL

BOTTOM & SIDE MEMBERS LAP... SCREW FASTEN WITH 2-1/4" #8 SCREWS

BOTTOM LAPS SIDE PLANKING TO ABOUT 30" FROM STEM

131

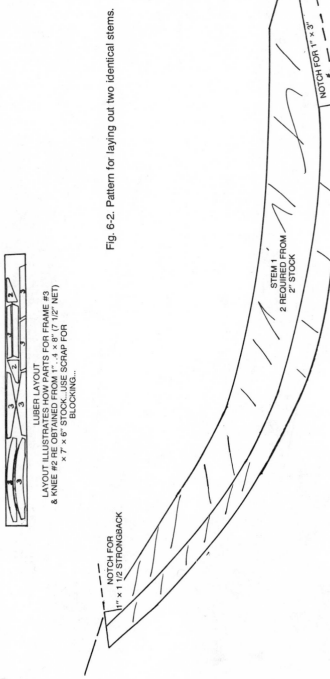

Fig. 6-2. Pattern for laying out two identical stems.

LUBER LAYOUT
LAYOUT ILLUSTRATES HOW PARTS FOR FRAME #3
& KNEE #2 RE OBTAINED FROM 1"...4 × 8' (7 1/2" NET)
× 7" × 6" STOCK...USE SCRAP FOR
BLOCKING...

STEM 1
2 REQUIRED FROM
2" STOCK

NOTCH FOR 1" × 3"

KEEL

NOTCH FOR
1" × 1 1/2 STRONGBACK

The two frames required for this kayak are identical and are constructed as shown in Fig. 6-1, using either oak, mahogany or spruce (1″ × 8″) lumber. Note that the side frame members lap both the bottom members and deck beam members. The side frame members are left extending above the deck beam members so they can be used for building purposes. They'll later be trimmed off. When assembling, coat the mating frame members with glue and fasten at each junction with two 1 1/2-inch wood screws. Then notch for chine, keel and sheer members as indicated. Be sure to measure the depth and width of each board before making a notch for it: board sizes vary from lumber yard to lumber yard. Your sabre saw will be ideal for notching, but a hand keyhole saw would work almost as well, requiring only a little more elbow grease.

You should cut out the two identical stems from 2″ × 6″ lumber yard material according to the drawing (Fig. 6-2). Since lumber yard material will finish out to a width of about 1 1/2 inches, two pieces of 3/4-inch plywood glued and fastened together with 1 1/4-inch screws will work just as well. Stagger these fasteners and space them about 6 inches apart. Then notch as shown for the strongback and keel members and pre-bevel the stem as shown in Fig. 6-3 to eliminate excessive fairing. Again, either the sabre or keyhole saw will be suitable for cutting out these members.

The 1″ × 3″ keel is 8 feet 4 inches long and tapered at each end from a point 6 inches from the end to a tapered width to match the thickness of the stem as shown in the framing detail in Fig. 6-4. Use bronze or hot dipped galvanized screws (1 1/2″ #8) to fasten the keel to the frames and the stem members. Use a minimum of two screws per frame member and three per stem member. Much work can be saved by pre-drilling the screw holes with a slightly under-sized drill bit and then drive the screws with either a ratchet screwdriver, a brace with a screwdriver bit, or a 1/4-inch electric drill with a screwdriver bit.

At each end of the craft a strongback joins the stem to the frame. The strongbacks are fitted into notches and secured with screws (1 1/2″ #8). During the building process, it would be preferable to leave the strongbacks as a single piece of lumber extending from one end to the other as shown in Fig. 6-5. Doing this will reinforce the stems and prevent distortion during the spring-in of

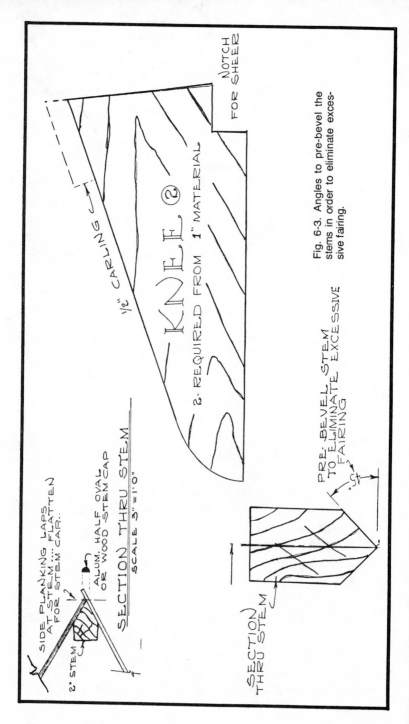

NOTCH FOR SHEER

½" CARLING

KNEE ②

2- REQUIRED FROM 1" MATERIAL

SIDE PLANKING LAPS AT STEM... FLATTEN FOR STEM CAP..

ALUM. HALF OVAL OR WOOD STEM CAP

2" STEM

SECTION THRU STEM

SCALE 3" = 1'0"

PRE-BEVEL STEM TO ELIMINATE EXCESSIVE FAIRING

SECTION THRU STEM

Fig. 6-3. Angles to pre-bevel the stems in order to eliminate excessive fairing.

the chine and sheers. Note in the illustration that the keel and strongback are straight and parallel to each other.

When gluing and securing the strongback to frames and stems, it is advisable to place cross braces between all frame members and between the end frame members and the stem. Use only nails for this; do not glue or use screws.

The chine is that member of the boat's frame that backs up the junction of the side and bottom planking. In this case, it runs completely from stem to stem and fits into the notches provided in the frames. Bevel these notches so that the chines will bear on the entire area and not just on one corner. To fit the chines at the stems, bend the chine into a smooth curve that steepens at the stem. Taper one end of the chine in a long bevel so it will fit to the side of the stem. Leave the opposite end long for fitting and springing around the hull form. Make a junction with the stem at the same point on the other end of the chine and taper the chine to fit, but do not cut off any excess. Coat each of the contact points with glue and fasten with 1 1/2-inch wood screws—two at the stem joints and one at the frames.

The sheer backs up the junction of the side planking and decking. This 1" × 1" member is similar to the chine and is also fitted into the notches provided in the two frames. It is then beveled to fit the side of the stem. In fact, the fitting of the sheer to the stems is almost identical to the fitting of the chines described previously.

This just about completes the basic framework of the kayak. Your boat now should look much like the one in Fig. 6-6.

We stated before that no building form is required for this particular craft. However, always work on a flat surface—floor, bench, or platform. Having such a surface to work on, you need only concern yourself with keeping the frames vertical, level, centered, and properly spaced. (Leveling should be done with the instrument placed on the inside of the bottom frame member.)

With the framework now completed, you're probably anxious to install the planking and get your project onto the water. However, before installing the planking, you must fair or bevel the framework so that the planking will lie flat and mate with all members. This means that fairing will be required primarily along the chine, sheer, stem and keel. Check with a length of plywood or scrap lumber from

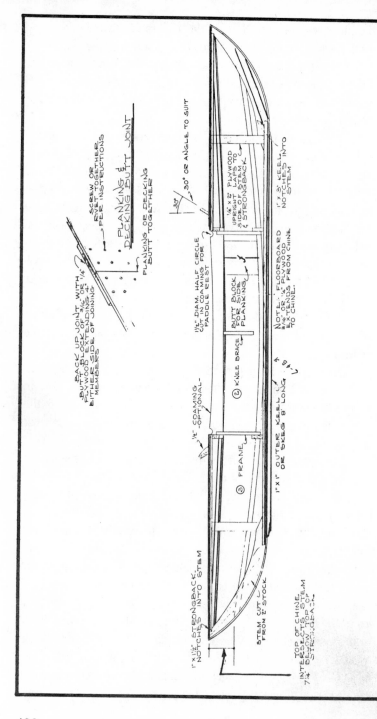

BACK UP JOINT WITH
BUTT BLOCK OF 3/16" OR 1/4"
PLYWOOD EXTENDING 4"
EITHER SIDE OF JOINING
MEMBERS OF JOINING

SCREW OR
RIVET TOGETHER
PER INSTRUCTIONS

PLANKING &
DECKING BUTT JOINT

PLANKING OR DECKING
BUTT TOGETHER

30° OR ANGLE TO SUIT

1/4" x 2" PLYWOOD
UPRIGHT LAPS TO
SIDE BEAM
& STRONGBACK

1" x 3" KEEL
NOTCHES INTO
STEM

11/2" DIAM. HALF CIRCLE
CUT IN COAMING FOR
PADDLE REST

BUTT BLOCK
FOR SIDE
PLANKING

NOTE: FLOORBOARD
3/16" OR 1/4" PLYWOOD
EXTENDS FROM CHINE
TO CHINE.

1/4" COAMING
OPTIONAL

② KNEE BRACE

1" x 1" OUTER KEEL
OR SKEG 8' LONG

7' - 8"

③ FRAME

1" x 11/2" STRONGBACK.
NOTCHES INTO STEM

STEM CUT
FROM 2" STOCK

TOP OF CHINE.
INTERSECTS STEM
71/4" BELOW TOP OF
STRONGBACK.

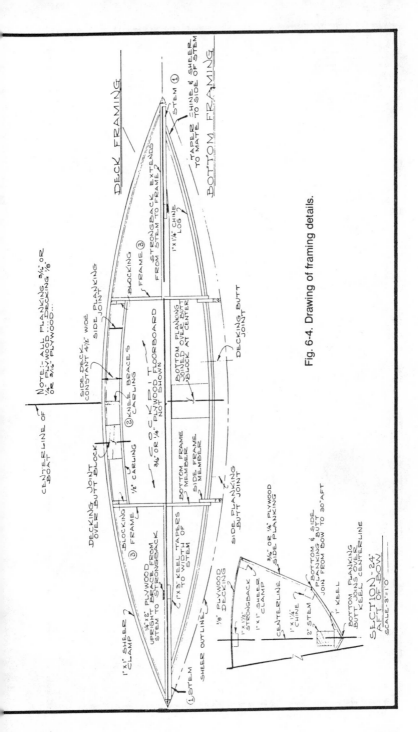

Fig. 6-4. Drawing of framing details.

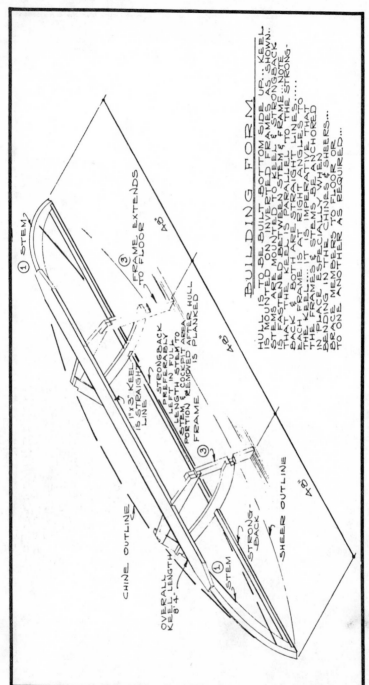

BUILDING FORM

HULL IS TO BE BUILT BOTTOM SIDE UP... KEEL IS MOUNTED ON INVERTED FRAMES AS SHOWN.. STRINGERS ARE MOUNTED TO KEEL & STRONGBACK IS FASTENED BETWEEN STEM & FRAME..NOTE THAT THE KEEL IS PARALLEL TO THE STRONGBACK & BOTH ARE STRAIGHT LINES..... EACH FRAME IS AT RIGHT ANGLES TO THE KEEL.... IT IS IMPERATIVE THAT THE FRAMES & STEMS BE ANCHORED IN PLACE ESPECIALLY WHEN BENDING IN THE CHINES & SHEERS... BRACE MEMBERS TO FLOOR OR TO ONE ANOTHER AS REQUIRED...

CHINE OUTLINE

OVERALL KEEL LENGTH 8' 4"

STEM ①

STRONG-BACK

SHEER OUTLINE

A"B"

A"B"

A"B"

① STEM

1"x3' KEEL IS STRAIGHT LINE

STRONGBACK PREFERABLY LEFT IN FULL LENGTH STEM TO STEM..COCKPIT AREA PORTION REMOVED AFTER HULL IS PLANKED

③ FRAME

③ FRAME EXTENDS TO FLOOR

Fig. 6-5. Pictorial drawing of framing details.

138

chine to sheer, starting at the midpoint and working outward to stem areas. Bevel the members so they'll mate solidly with the planking and not simply rest on one edge. You will also have to check and bevel between the other members—along the stem and elsewhere.

You'll have to make a transition joint at each end of the planking—along the chine about 30 inches from the terminus. (This procedure will be explained in the section on the installation of planking.) The chine should be beveled from the center of the hull outward to the transition joints. From this point draw a line to the center of the chine where the chine meets the stem. The area above this line must be faired for the bottom planking; the area below this line will become the mating surface for the side planking. The beveling for the bottom planking will diminish gradually in the direction of the stem. At the stem proper, little if any fairing should be required. Similarly, little or no material will have to be removed for the side planking anywhere along the chine. Figure 6-7 shows how to determine the amount of beveling necessary.

All of the lines must be clean even sweeps without humps. You can use a wood rasp or sander on short spans, but always finish up the long sweeps along the keel, chine, and sheer with a plane. You

Fig. 6-6. Appearance of kayak after the completion of the basic frame work.

Fig. 6-7. Beveling the frame work so the planking will lie flat to all surfaces.

also may have to remove some material from the frames to keep them from coming into contact with the planking—either on the sides or bottom. Since the planking in this vicinity won't be fastened, a projecting frame will stand out like a sore thumb.

The layout of the planking is detailed in the drawings of Fig. 6-8. Extremely thrifty cutting will be necessary if you are to obtain all of the members from the listed materials. Thickness of the (exterior) plywood planking can be 3/16 inch or 1/4 inch. (The 3/16-inch size may be difficult to find but every lumber yard will have bins full of 1/4-inch 4′ × 8′ sheets.) Butt joints in all planking should be united with a butt block of the same thickness as the planking and extending at least 4 inches on either side of the joint. The butt block should be fastened with 5/8″ #7 brass screws or 3/4-inch nails placed in two rows on either side of the joint and spaced not more than 2 inches apart. If screws are used, the projecting points on the inside should be peened over or filed smooth; if nails are used, the tips should be clinched over. All butt joints should be coated liberally with glue prior to fastening. Such joints derive more of their strength from the glue bond than from the metal fasteners. A butt block may be installed on a panel before the panel is butted to its mate; the block would then be

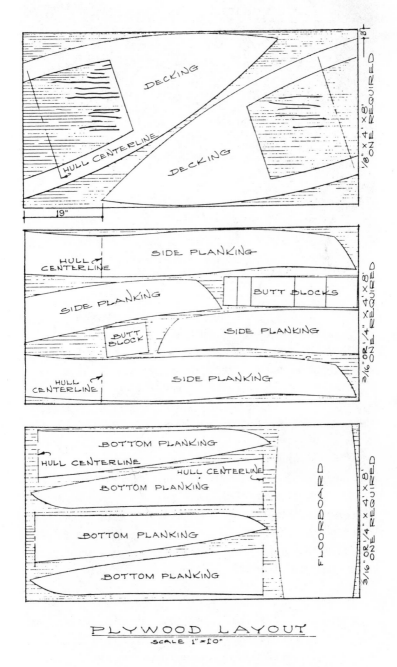

Fig. 6-8. Layout of the planking members on the sheets of plywood.

141

Fig. 6-9. Paper may be wrapped around the side of the hull and trimmed along the stem, chine, and sheer for use as a template to cut planking.

fastened to the mating panel. Further, the builder has the option of completing his butt joints before fastening the planking to the hull.

Note in Fig. 6-4 that the pattern of butt joints is the same on each side of the craft: the bottom planking panels join at the midline; the side planking panels and the decking panels are joined fore and aft of the midline, respectively. If side planking is joined fore of midline on the port side, it will be joined aft of midline on the starboard side. The same principle of staggering joints applies to the joining of deck panels.

The side planking need only be carefully fitted along the chine from the bow back for a distance of about 30 inches. Paper may be wrapped around the side of the hull (Fig. 6-9) and trimmed along the stem, chine and sheer for use as a template to cut this planking. At the center the planking may be left long and trimmed to fit after it is fastened in place. Rough cut the side planking for an approximate fit and then clamp in place (Fig. 6-10) for scribing and final cutting and fitting.

Now fit the side planking along the chine from a point about 30 inches from the bow aft, coating all of the mating surfaces with glue and fastening the side planking to the chine and sheer with 3/4-inch wood screws spaced 3 inches apart along the chine and 4 inches apart along the sheer. Along the stem areas use 1″ #8 wood screws

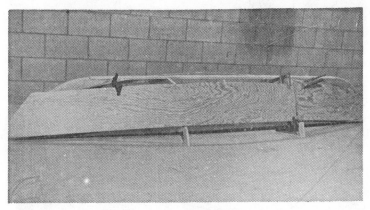

Fig. 6-10. Here planking is rough-cut and clamped.

spaced about 2 inches apart. After fastening the initial panel in place, trim all overhanging edges except along the sheer. At the bow this panel will be lapped by the panel on the opposite side (Fig. 6-11).

With the side planking securely in place, go on to the bottom planking, applying the panels in halves on either side of the center-line. Rest the panel on the bottom and mark roughly around the extremities. Fit along the center of the keel first and then carefully along the chine so that this portion will buttjoin with the side plank-

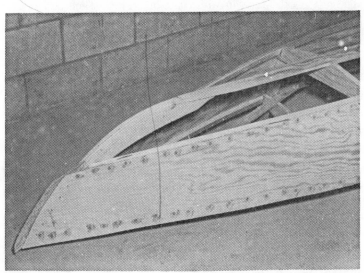

Fig. 6-11. Observe how the initial sheet of plywood is lapped by the other side at the stem.

Fig. 6-12. Bottom planking of the kayak fitted into place.

ing. In the center between these points, the bottom planking will lap the side planking, but not at the transition point mentioned earlier. To mark the area from the bow to the transition point, coat the sharp edge of the side planking with chalk or crayola. Then bump the bottom panel on this edge to transfer the line to the panel's underside. Cut slightly away from this line and plane carefully to insure precise butting to the side planking. When doing so, coat the mating areas with glue and screw to the chine and keel with wood screws (3/4" #8) spaced about 3 inches apart. Along the stem use 1" #8 screws spaced about 2 inches apart. Trim the overhang along the stems and where the bottom planking laps the side planking. The opposite side of the bottom will buttjoin the initially applied panel above the keel centerline, but its edge will have to be beveled if it is to mate properly. Actually, a slight gap won't be serious since the skeg and bow trim cover the entire area from stem to stem. Figure 6-12 shows the bottom planking fitted in place. The blocks in this illustration are used as washers under the screw heads to prevent the fastenings from tearing through the plywood.

The skeg—sometimes referred to as the outer keel—is 1" × 1" × 8' and covers the seam over the bottom planking on the

144

keel centerline. It will be necessary to flatten the plywood planking so the skeg will bear solidly. Coat the skeg liberally with glue, lay in place, and secure with 1 1/2″ #8 wood screws spaced about 6 inches apart.

You may want to apply a fiberglass covering to the bottom of this craft (instructions are given in Chapter 9). In this case, the outer skeg will not be put on until after the fiberglass coating has been applied and it will be imbedded in the resin.

If the hull is fiberglassed, the stem cap can be eliminated, although it is still recommended. This half oval cap is best if made of aluminum or brass, but one of oak or other hardwood would also serve well. The cap will extend from the deck to the skeg.

The hull should now be righted as shown in Fig. 6-13. Make certain that the inner members of the frame are level and chocked in the illustrated position. The protruding frame ends are now cut off and the sheer area trimmed to achieve a smooth flowing curve.

Before installing the decking, you will have to insert the deck uprights and the carling. The uprights are merely pieces of 1/4-inch plywood about 2 inches wide extending from the side of the stem to the side of the strongback on both ends of the boat. When installing,

Fig. 6-13. Hull is righted and chocked in this position for further work.

Fig. 6-14. Upright brace of 1/4-inch plywood extends from keel-stem area to strongback to reinforce the decking area.

make certain that the strongback line is straight and true; then fasten uprights with glue and 3/4-inch nails.

The carling members extend between the frames and form the sides of the cockpit. As indicated in the previous drawings, the carlings are set 4 1/2 inches to the inside of the sheer clamps and follow the same arcs. Now support the frames with blocking and install the knee (cut from the template) on the centerline of the boat. Then spring the carling in place, temporarily leaving it about 3 inches below the deck level at each of the frames. The top edge of the carling will have to be cut in an arc to conform to the contour of the sheer as seen in profile. It is advisable to rough cut the carling before installation but the final trimming and beveling should be done after the member is permanently set. Fasten the carling to all other members with 1 1/2" #8 screws (two at each contact point) after having coated the mating surfaces with glue. Figure 6-14 shows the 1/4-inch upright extending from the keel/stem junction to the strongback in order to reinforce the decking area.

The entire deck area should be trimmed and faired to provide positive mating surfaces for the plywood decking. This fairing operation will be similar to that done on the planking. The interior of the boat should be painted before the deck planking is installed, because afterward the bow areas are difficult to reach.

Figure 6-15 shows that the decking extends from sheer to sheer. It is preferable to use 1/8-inch plywood for the decking, but if this thickness is not available at your supply house, 1/4-inch may be used. Of course, the weight of the boat will be increased.

Butt blocks are used for the decking as they were for the side planking. One-quarter inch plywood is the best choice for these blocks, no matter the thickness of the decking. Coat all mating areas with glue and fasten the decking at its borders with 3/4-inch nails spaced 2 inches apart. Fastening is optional on the decking's inner areas, but if fasteners are used along the strongback, they should be well staggered and spaced 6 inches apart.

As shown on the drawings, a capping member (a rail) is used to cover the exposed edge of the decking where it laps the side planking. The rail will be 5/8-inch half oval, either aluminum or hardwood. Even a flat strip would do.

Your boat at this time should look somewhat like the one in Fig. 6-16. Note that the grain of the cockpit's floorboards runs athwart-

Fig. 6-15. Decking in forward area extends from sheer to sheer with layout approximately as shown in the drawings.

Fig. 6-16. Cockpit area illustrating floor boards with grain running athwartship. Blocking is provided in center over keel to support floorboards.

ship. Note also that blocking is provided in the center over the keel to support the floorboards.

To improve your craft's ability to withstand the bumps which can cause minor leaks, you can strengthen the bottom of the hull with fiberglass. Follow the directions given in Chapter 9 and apply the material to the bare wood surface prior to the installation of any of the appendages such as skeg, stem, cap, bumper rail, etc.

The splash boards, also called coamings, are cut from 1/2-inch mahogany or similar wood. The bottom edge of each splash board is level with the carling while the top edge projects above the deck— about 1 1/4 inches at the midpoint and 2 inches at the ends. The splash boards, one fore and one aft of the cockpit, are canted 30 degrees to the vertical, their upper edges angled toward the stems.

The floorboard of 1/4-inch plywood will extend between the frames from chine to chine; it will rest on the keel at centerline and touch against the bottom planking at the sides. The floorboard should be removable, so fasten it down only over the keel. Place countersunk washers under the screw heads. Life preserver cushions can serve for kneeling or sitting pads.

148

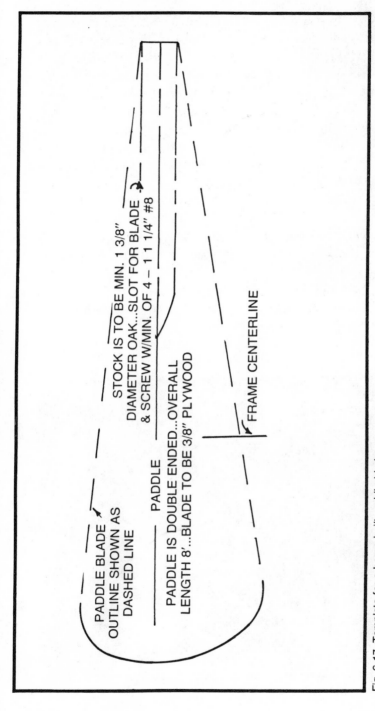

STOCK IS TO BE MIN. 1 3/8"
DIAMETER OAK...SLOT FOR BLADE
& SCREW W/MIN. OF 4 – 1 1 1/4" #8

PADDLE BLADE
OUTLINE SHOWN AS
DASHED LINE

PADDLE

PADDLE IS DOUBLE ENDED...OVERALL
LENGTH 8'...BLADE TO BE 3/8" PLYWOOD

FRAME CENTERLINE

Fig. 6-17. Template for a home-built paddle blade.

149

The painting of the craft is the final step before trying her out on your favorite river or lake. If you decide to fiberglass the hull, you should use paint which is compatible with this material. All fir plywood surfaces not to be fiberglassed should be treated with a plywood sealer and primed with a flat marine paint. Sand between coats until the grain is hidden. Finish off with two coats of marine enamel in any appropriate color. If you desire to leave some of the wood—like the mahogany splash boards—in a natural finish, it should be filler stained to the desired tone and given a minimum of three coats of marine varnish.

You will find that double-ended paddles—just like the ones the Eskimos use—will be best for this craft for most applications. A double-ended paddle may be purchased at your local sporting goods or boating supply store, but since you've come this far, why not build your own?

A template for the paddle blade is given in Fig. 6-17. The handle is 1 3/8 inches in diameter and would be best if made from oak. Dowel stock, the kind used for clothes closet rods, makes an excellent handle. Slot the ends of the handle to fit the paddle blade as

Fig. 6-18. Slot the ends of dowel stock for the paddle blade and then glue and screw in place.

Fig. 6-19. One of the pleasures derived from the finished product.

shown in Fig. 6-18 and then glue and screw in place. The paddle blades should be made of 3/8-inch plywood, but 1/2-inch will suffice.

Figure 6-19 shows why the builder derives such deep satisfaction from his labors. The completed product will be an enduring source of pleasure and pride, provided that he abides by the hints and suggestions given in Chapter 10.

# The Bass Fisherman's Delight

While a little more complicated than the designs previously discussed, this bass boat is not out of reach of the average handyman—especially if he uses the readymade frame kit and full size patterns available for less than $150 from Glen L Marine Designs, 9152 Rosecrans, Bellflower, Calif. 90706. The end result will be a $1500 boat for less than $500, plus about 120 hours or so of your time.

Check over the deck layout of this boat in Fig. 7-1 and you'll readily see that this design contains just about everything that even the most self-indulgent bass fisherman could desire. Of course, you won't get all of these "gadgets" for the $500 mentioned earlier—that was just the cost of the hull—but the bundle of dough you'll save by building the hull yourself will go a long way toward buying these accessories and maybe some fancy lures to boot.

The craft has an overall length of 15 feet 5 inches and a generous beam width of 5 feet 4 inches. The cockpit is 11 feet 4 inches long. The hull can handle short or long shaft outboard motors up to 70 HP with no risk. On open throttle, the boat rides easy and flat; at rest, it has plenty of reserve stability for steady casting. You can operate the boat from the control console where the electronic fish finder and water temperature indicator are located—along with compass, spotlight, steering wheel, and other gauges. On the other hand, you might prefer to omit the control console, and use the

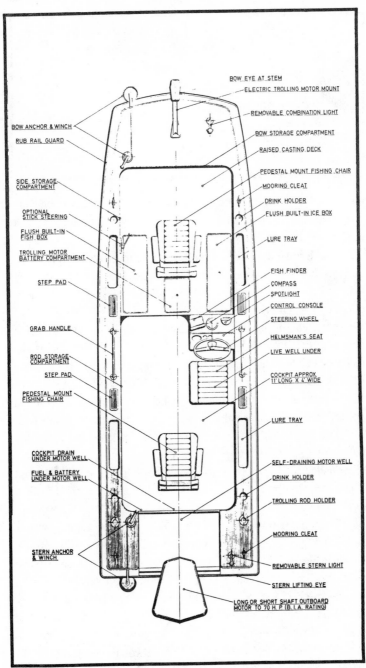

**BOW EYE AT STEM**
**ELECTRIC TROLLING MOTOR MOUNT**
**REMOVABLE COMBINATION LIGHT**
**BOW STORAGE COMPARTMENT**
**RAISED CASTING DECK**
**PEDESTAL MOUNT FISHING CHAIR**
**MOORING CLEAT**
**DRINK HOLDER**
**FLUSH BUILT-IN ICE BOX**
**LURE TRAY**
**FISH FINDER**
**COMPASS**
**SPOTLIGHT**
**CONTROL CONSOLE**
**STEERING WHEEL**
**HELMSMAN'S SEAT**
**LIVE WELL UNDER**
**COCKPIT APPROX. 11' LONG X 4' WIDE**
**LURE TRAY**
**SELF-DRAINING MOTOR WELL**
**DRINK HOLDER**
**TROLLING ROD HOLDER**
**MOORING CLEAT**
**REMOVABLE STERN LIGHT**
**STERN LIFTING EYE**
**LONG OR SHORT SHAFT OUTBOARD MOTOR TO 70 H.P. (B.I.A. RATING)**

**BOW ANCHOR & WINCH**
**RUB RAIL GUARD**
**SIDE STORAGE COMPARTMENT**
**OPTIONAL STICK STEERING**
**FLUSH BUILT-IN FISH BOX**
**TROLLING MOTOR BATTERY COMPARTMENT**
**STEP PAD**
**GRAB HANDLE**
**ROD STORAGE COMPARTMENT**
**STEP PAD**
**PEDESTAL MOUNT FISHING CHAIR**
**COCKPIT DRAIN UNDER MOTOR WELL**
**FUEL & BATTERY UNDER MOTOR WELL**
**STERN ANCHOR & WINCH**

Fig. 7-1. Plan view of bass boat showing layout of pedestal chairs, anchors, control console, and other accessories.

153

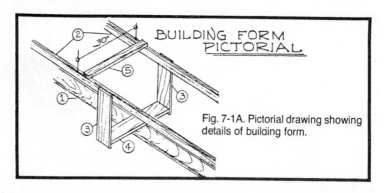

BUILDING FORM PICTORIAL

Fig. 7-1A. Pictorial drawing showing details of building form.

popular stick steering control instead. That's the beauty of building your own boat...you can build it just the way you want it, and you'll save a wad by doing so.

The lightweight (425 pounds) super-strong plywood construction lets this bass boat be trailered with ease. One person can easily load and unload this craft at conventional boat landings. Even in difficult-to-reach areas, it'll only take two.

A dedicated bass fisherman must have the best equipment if he consistently is to find the lunker bass, and what's more important, make them bite! That's what this bass boat is all about. It's just the right length, just the right beam, just the right depth, just the right size to carry all of your equipment. It'll take plenty of power too, so you won't have to spend all day getting to where the big ones are.

This boat can even be a money-maker for you. Many persons living alongside or near good bass waters use such a craft to "guide" other fishermen to where the big ones are. For your boat, gear, and ability to make the fish bite, clients are willing to pay around $75 a day...and you'll get to fish, too!

This boat is to be built bottom side up with a building form as shown in Fig. 7-1A. The boat members are arranged on the form as shown in Fig. 7-2. Member No. 1, the base member, is a single piece of 2″ × 6″ × 14′ lumber. The set up members (No. 2) consist of two pieces of 2″ × 4″ × 7′ lumber which must be installed perfectly level—both lengthwise and athwartship. The leg uprights (No. 3) consist of four pieces of 1″ × 6″ × 2′ lumber. The two leg spreaders (No. 4) are each 2″ × 6″ × 30″. The three frame cleats (No. 5) are each 2″ × 4″ × 36″. This completes the bill of materials for the building form.

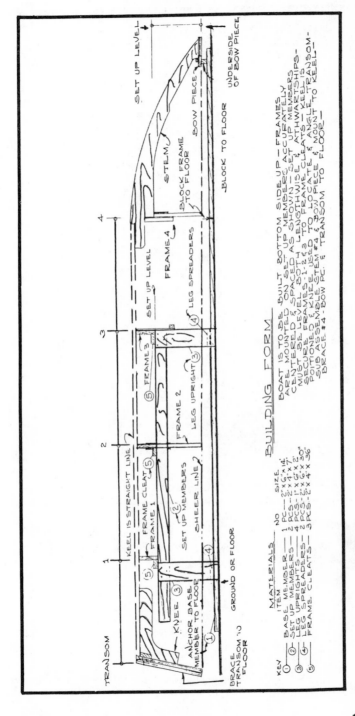

Fig. 7-2. Elevation of building form showing placement of transom, stem, and frames.

155

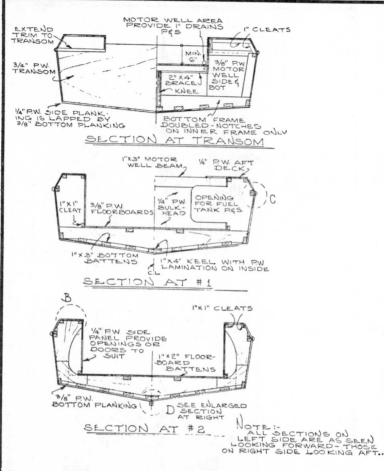

Fig. 7-3. Sectional drawings of transom and frames.

At this point, you may wish to purchase a ready-made frame kit for this boat to make the building go faster and easier. The kit sells for around $130 and includes the following:

1. Transom (fully framed)
2. Frames (preassembled)
3. Transom knee
4. Stem
5. Bow piece
6. Complete plans, bill of materials and fastening schedule.

156

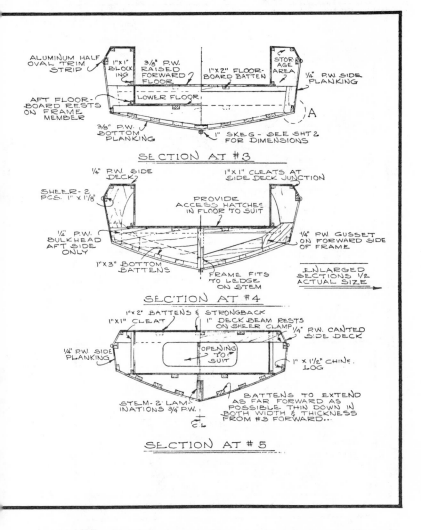

ALUMINUM HALF OVAL TRIM STRIP
1"×1" BLOCKING
3/8" P.W. RAISED FORWARD FLOOR
1"×2" FLOORBOARD BATTEN
STORAGE AREA
1/4" P.W. SIDE PLANKING
AFT FLOORBOARD RESTS ON FRAME MEMBER
LOWER FLOOR
A
3/8" P.W. BOTTOM PLANKING
1" SKEG - SEE SHT 2 FOR DIMENSIONS

SECTION AT #3

1/4" P.W. SIDE DECK
1"×1" CLEATS AT SIDE DECK JUNCTION
SHEER - 2 PCS. 1" × 1 1/8"
PROVIDE ACCESS HATCHES IN FLOOR TO SUIT
1/4" P.W. BULKHEAD AFT SIDE ONLY
1/4" P.W. GUSSET ON FORWARD SIDE OF FRAME
1"×3" BOTTOM BATTENS
FRAME FITS TO LEDGE ON STEM
ENLARGED SECTIONS 1/2 ACTUAL SIZE

SECTION AT #4

1"×2" BATTENS & STRONGBACK
1"×1" CLEAT
1" DECK BEAM RESTS ON SHEER CLAMP
1/4" P.W. CANTED SIDE DECK
1/4" P.W. SIDE PLANKING
OPENING TO SUIT
1" × 1 1/2" CHINE LOG
STEM - 2 LAMINATIONS 3/4" P.W.
BATTENS TO EXTEND AS FAR FORWARD AS POSSIBLE. THIN DOWN IN BOTH WIDTH & THICKNESS FROM #3 FORWARD...
CL

SECTION AT #5

Sections of the transom and the various frames are shown in Fig. 7-3. Details of these sections—A, B, C, and D—are shown in Fig. 7-4. The details show how the joints are properly made, even indicating the angles of the various cuts.

Refer again to Fig. 7-2 to continue construction after the framing members have been obtained. Secure frames 1, 2, and 3 to frame cleats as shown in the drawing. Next position the 1″ × 4″ keel in a straight line across the frame. Note in section D of Fig. 7-4 that a lamination of 1/4-inch plywood is required on the inside of the keel.

Fig. 7-4A. Detail drawing showing the joining of 1/4-inch side planking with 3/8-inch bottom planking by means of a chine log.

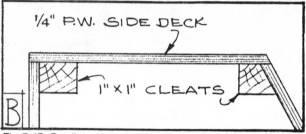

Fig. 7-4B. Detail drawing of construction of side deck.

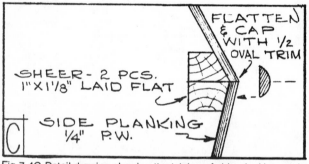

Fig. 7-4C. Detail drawing showing the joining of side planking angles.

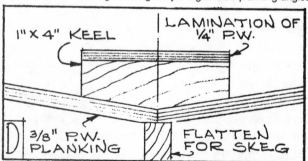

Fig. 7-4D. Detail drawing of vee bottom showing method of fairing keel and flattening bottom planking for the skeg.

The transom knee is then glued and secured (with wood screws) to the keel to locate and angle the transom. When this step has been completed, brace the transom to the floor. Finish up this part of the construction by assembling frame 4 and bow piece and mount both to the keel with glue and wood screws. Then brace the bow piece to the floor or base member. The keel itself fastens to the stem with two 3/8-inch carriage bolts.

At this point make certain that all framing members are plumb, correctly spaced, and perfectly level. Then begin positioning the 1″ × 3″ battens, the 1″ × 1 1/2″ chine logs, the 1″ × 1″ cleats, and the 1″ × 1 1/8″ sheers on the bottom and sides of the framing members. Refer to Figs. 7-5 and 7-6 for further details.

Once all the framing members have been positioned and secured, it will be necessary to bevel or fair the framework so that the planking will lie flat to all surfaces. Shaping will be necessary along the keel and chines for the bottom planking. You can make a template for cutting the planking by wrapping paper around the sides and bottom of the hull, then trimming the paper neatly. Now rough cut the side planking panels and clamp them in place for final scribing and cutting to an exact fit.

Next comes the bottom planking. It is rough cut, scribed, and precisely fitted in the same fashion as the side planking. The 3/8-inch bottom planking and the 1/4-inch side planking are then coated with a hard setting glue at all mating surfaces and secured in place with hot dipped galvanized or bronze wood screws at intervals recommended by the kit's fastening schedule.

After all planking is installed and firmly secured, fill screw heads, holes, and cracks with a waterproof wood putty. Then right the hull and begin the interior work; that is, the floor boards, motorwell, helm, seats, and ice and fish containers.

Until now you have had to follow instructions right to a tee, but at this point you have room to vary the construction of the boat as much as you'd like.

Basically, you'll want to equip your new bass boat with two pedestal-mount, swivel fishing chairs—one forward and one aft. Perhaps you'll want stick steering at the forward position, or maybe the regular control console will suffice—especially since you're certain to have an electric trolling motor on the bow anyway.

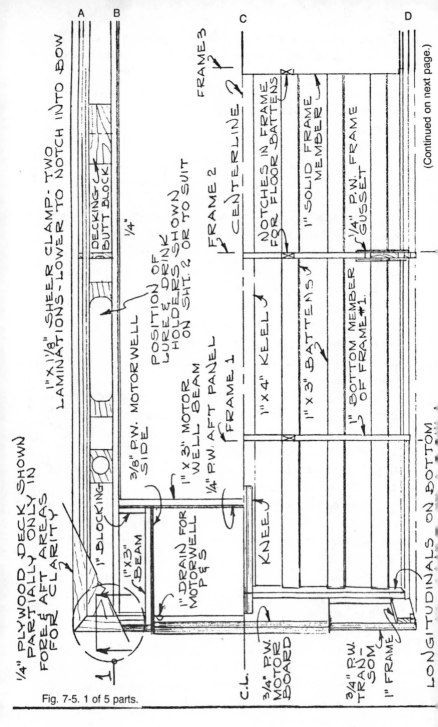

Fig. 7-5. 1 of 5 parts.

(Continued on next page.)

160

(Continued from previous page.)

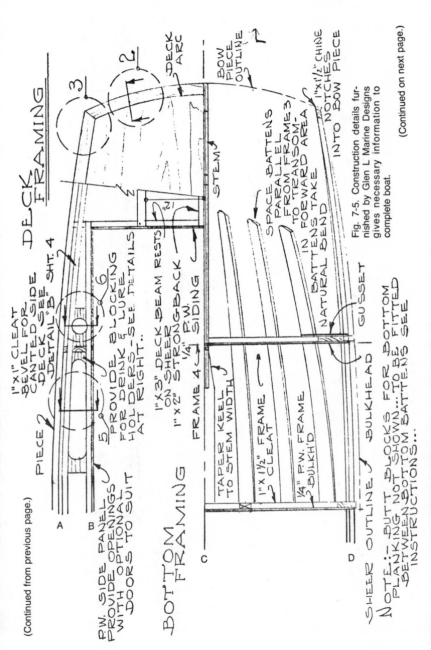

DECK FRAMING

1"x1" CLEAT
CANTED SIDE
BEVEL FOR DECK SEE
DETAIL "B" SHT. 4

DECK ARC

BOW PIECE OUTLINE

PIECE 2

P.W. SIDE PANEL
PROVIDE OPENINGS
WITH OPTIONAL
DOORS TO SUIT

PROVIDE BLOCKING
FOR DRINK & LURE
HOLDERS—SEE DETAILS
AT RIGHT..

SPACE BATTENS
PARALLEL
FROM FRAME 3
TO TRANSOM—
FORWARD AREA

STEM

1"x1/2" CHINE
NOTCHES
INTO BOW PIECE

BATTENS TAKE
IN NATURAL BEND

BOTTOM FRAMING

1"x3" DECK BEAM RESTS
ON SHEER
1"x2" P.W. SIDING
1/4" STRONGBACK

FRAME 4

TAPER KEEL
TO STEM WIDTH

1"x1½" FRAME
CLEAT

1/4" P.W. FRAME
BULKH'D

GUSSET

SHEER OUTLINE

BULKHEAD

NOTE:- BUTT BLOCKS FOR BOTTOM
PLANKING NOT SHOWN...TO BE FITTED
BETWEEN BOTTOM BATTENS SEE
INSTRUCTIONS...

Fig. 7-5. Construction details furnished by Glen L Marine Designs
gives necessary information to
complete boat.

(Continued on next page.)

161

(Continued from previous page.)

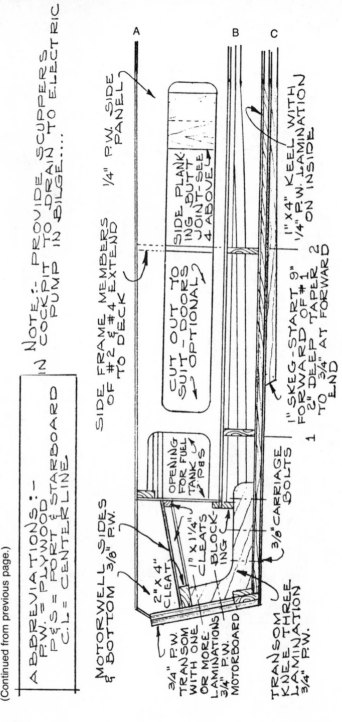

ABBREVIATIONS:-
P.W. = PLYWOOD
P&S = PORT & STARBOARD
C.L. = CENTERLINE

NOTE:- PROVIDE SCUPPERS
IN COCKPIT TO DRAIN TO ELECTRIC
PUMP IN BILGE....

1/4" P.W. SIDE PANEL

SIDE FRAME MEMBERS
OF #2 & #4 EXTEND
TO DECK

SIDE PLANKING BUTT
JOINT—SEE 4 ABOVE

CUT OUT TO
SUIT—DOORS
OPTIONAL

1" x 4" KEEL WITH
1/4" P.W. LAMINATION
ON INSIDE

1" SKEG—START 9"
FORWARD OF #1
2" DEEP TAPER 2
TO 3/4" AT FORWARD
END

OPENING
FOR FUEL
TANK P&S

MOTORWELL SIDES &
BOTTOM 3/8" P.W.

2" x 4"
CLEAT

1" X 1 1/4"
CLEATS
BLOCK-
ING

3/4" P.W.
TRANSOM
WITH ONE
OR MORE
LAMINATIONS
3/4" P.W.
MOTORBOARD

3/8" CARRIAGE
BOLTS

TRANSOM
KNEE THREE
LAMINATION
3/4" P.W.

(Continued on next page.)

162

(Continued from previous page.)

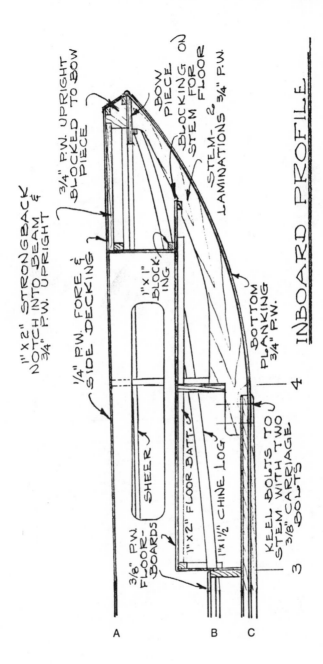

INBOARD PROFILE

(Continued on next page.)

Fig. 7-5. 2 of 5 parts.

163

(Continued from previous page.)

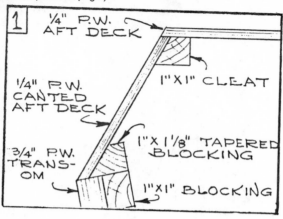

1  ¼" P.W. AFT DECK
1"X1" CLEAT
¼" P.W. CANTED AFT DECK
1"X1⅛" TAPERED BLOCKING
¾" P.W. TRANSOM
1"X1" BLOCKING

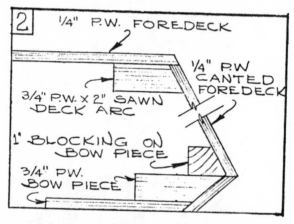

2  ¼" P.W. FOREDECK
¼" P.W CANTED FOREDECK
¾" P.W. X 2" SAWN DECK ARC
1" BLOCKING ON BOW PIECE
¾" P.W. BOW PIECE

3  NOTE:- DECK OMITTED FOR CLARITY
BEVEL FOR CANTED DECK
1"X1" SEE SECTION ON SHT 4 - DETAIL "B"
¾" P.W. X 2" SAWN DECK ARC

Fig. 7-5. 3 of 5 parts.

(Continued on next page.)

(Continued from previous page.)

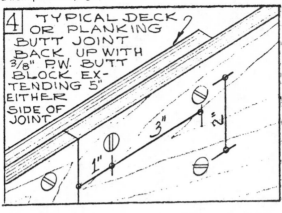

4 TYPICAL DECK OR PLANKING BUTT JOINT BACK UP WITH 3/8" P.W. BUTT BLOCK EXTENDING 5" EITHER SIDE OF JOINT

3"  2"  1"

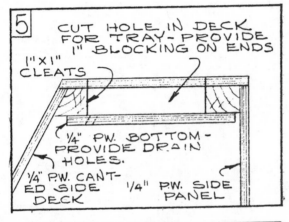

5 CUT HOLE IN DECK FOR TRAY-PROVIDE 1" BLOCKING ON ENDS

1"X1" CLEATS

1/4" P.W. BOTTOM-PROVIDE DRAIN HOLES.

1/4" P.W. CANTED SIDE DECK

1/4" P.W. SIDE PANEL

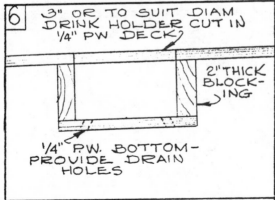

6 3" OR TO SUIT DIAM DRINK HOLDER CUT IN 1/4" PW DECK

2" THICK BLOCKING

1/4" P.W. BOTTOM—PROVIDE DRAIN HOLES

Fig. 7-5. 4 of 5 parts.

(Continued on next page.)

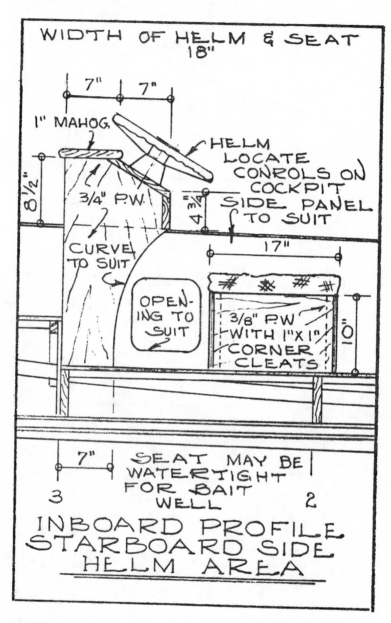

WIDTH OF HELM & SEAT
18"

7"    7"

1" MAHOG.

8½"

3/4" P.W.

HELM
LOCATE
CONROLS ON
COCKPIT
SIDE PANEL
TO SUIT

4 3/4"

CURVE
TO SUIT

OPEN-
ING TO
SUIT

17"

3/8" P.W
WITH 1"X1"
CORNER
CLEATS

10"

7"    SEAT MAY BE
WATERTIGHT
FOR BAIT
WELL

3                          2

INBOARD PROFILE
STARBOARD SIDE
HELM AREA

Fig. 7-5. 5 of 5 parts.

Two mushroom-type anchors will suffice for most bass fishing, but make sure that both can be controlled from where you're operating the craft; that is, forward or center. Anchor lines should lead from this position to rewind mechanisms at port and starboard.

If you'll refer again to Fig. 7-1, you'll see that the top surface of each gunwale is installed with a series of handy little recesses. Some are intended to hold drinks, others to hold lures and assorted fishing gear. Storage compartments lined with foam rubber and large enough to hold six or eight fishing rods can be built under the gunwales. Ice box, fish box, and trolling motor battery compartment are mounted flush beneath the forward deck. There's room for a storage locker in the bow and—if you need it—considerable extra space under the gunwale along each side.

Check with the local authorities to learn which accessories are prescribed by regulations. On most waters a boat of this size will be required to have such safety features as bow and stern lights, a spotlight, and perhaps a horn. If you have trouble judging how fast you're moving across the boat basin, then you'll need a speedometer.

Among the other optional accessories are compass, electronic fish finder/depth sounder, electronic water temperature gauge, tachometer, and battery gauge. The list goes on and on. But just how many of these accessories will you find truly necessary?

If you're going to be using the boat only on small rivers and streams, then you probably could dispense with a compass. However, if the craft will be used on the larger inland lakes where you could lose your direction in darkness or heavy fog, then a compass would be a necessity. A tachometer? Probably not. A battery condition gauge is a nice fillip, but with two batteries already on board, and an electric-starting outboard motor to charge them, this may be a wasted $15 – $20.

Those of you who are already hooked on bass fishing have more than likely heard of the electronic fish finders on the market— they're often referred to as depth sounders. But perhaps you haven't got around to using one yet. Now that you have a new bass boat—like the one described in this chapter—it's time to investigate the possibility of installing a fish finder.

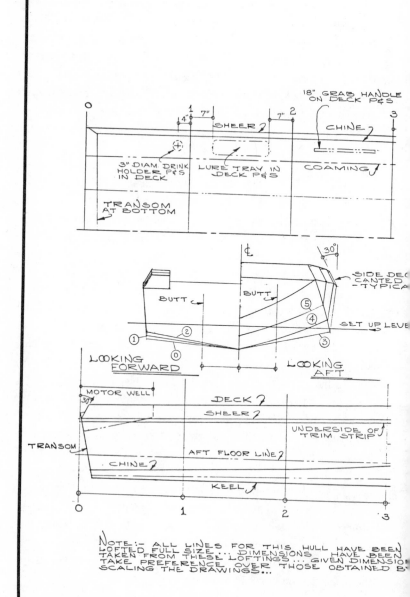

0    $\frac{1}{4}$" 7"   SHEER    7" 2    18" GRAB HANDLE
                                          ON DECK P&S
         4"                      CHINE               3

3" DIAM. DRINK     LURE TRAY IN      COAMING
HOLDER P&S         DECK P&S
IN DECK

TRANSOM
AT BOTTOM

                                          30°
                                                SIDE DECK
                                                CANTED
BUTT          BUTT                              - TYPICAL
                              ⑤
                              ④        SET UP LEVEL
① ②                           ③
        ⓪
LOOKING                    LOOKING
FORWARD                    AFT

MOTOR WELL
30°              DECK
                 SHEER
                              UNDERSIDE OF
TRANSOM                       TRIM STRIP
                 AFT FLOOR LINE
     CHINE
              KEEL

0         1              2            3

NOTE:- ALL LINES FOR THIS HULL HAVE BEEN
LOFTED FULL SIZE... DIMENSIONS HAVE BEEN
TAKEN FROM THESE LOFTINGS ... GIVEN DIMENSIO
TAKE PREFERENCE OVER THOSE OBTAINED B'
SCALING THE DRAWINGS...

# 'BASS BOAT'

## PARTICULARS....

LENGTH OVERALL ...15' 5".
BEAM MAXIMUM .........64".
HULL DEPTH MAX.......26".
MAXIMUM H.P ...........70

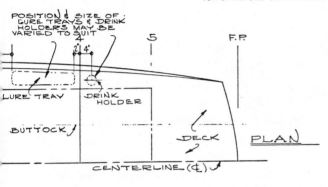

POSITION & SIZE OF
LURE TRAYS & DRINK
HOLDERS MAY BE
VARIED TO SUIT

4

5

F.P

LURE TRAY     DRINK
              HOLDER

BUTTOCK /

DECK     PLAN

CENTERLINE (₵)

NOTE:-
P & S REFERS TO PORT & STARBOARD

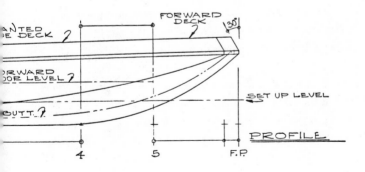

ANTED
DE DECK

FORWARD
DECK          30°

ORWARD
OOR LEVEL

SET UP LEVEL

BUTT

PROFILE

4          5          F.P

Fig. 7-6. Drawings show further details for construction of bass boat.

169

The signal receiving portion of the sonar fish finder can be mounted in the instrument control panel; this is the viewing end of the instrument and most dials are designed so that they can be adjusted for reading from any angle. The remote control transducer holder can be mounted on the transom or directly on the bottom of the boat if desired. Mounted on the bottom, it will give you fish and depth readings in a full 360-degree circle around your boat. A shielded cable connects the transducer to the signal receiving instrument.

The device will tell you the exact depth of the water and the nature of the floor—whether sandy, rocky, brushy, or weedy—essential information if you want consistent catches in unfamiliar waters. The dial will indicate the exact depth of the fish, too. Here's how the instrument works.

When the fish finder is on and operating, you will see two blips—one for the water surface, the other for the floor. Blips occurring between the two are the signal that a school of fish is passing beneath the boat. (An object with a configuration and density similar to a school's could produce a spurious signal.) With certain models of fish finders, you don't even have to monitor the screen since an audible alarm announces each find with a series of "bleeps."

A bottom alarm is a refinement featured by some of the better models. This alarm can be adjusted for any depth from 5 to 50 feet and will sound each time a blip is received from a depth less than the depth you preset on the dial. Obviously this model could be used as an alarm to guard against running aground or striking a rock or other subsurface obstacle. The alarm could also be used to locate underwater objects and to follow ledges and drop-offs.

Since fish are rarely found in water with a dissolved oxygen content of less than 5 PPM (parts per million) or more than 13 PPM, an electronic oxygen-content meter can be used by fishermen to identify waters where they'll have the best chance of finding their quarry. The meter, which can be installed in the control panel, is connected to a hundred feet or so of woven copper wire with an oxygen probe on the end. The probe is lowered to the desired depth and a dial at the control panel gives the reading.

Another device with an extensible sensor is the electronic thermometer. A dial on deck displays the temperature at various depths as transmitted through the cable attached to the sensor. Every species of fish has a temperature preference, and the electronic thermometer should make it easier to locate the one that interests you.

You may want to build a waterproof compartment (perhaps under the bow deck) for stowing such items as rain jacket, extension cord for battery charger, sealed beam spotlight, candy bars, and other snacks. This might also be a fine place for storing your camera and film.

A small tool box with extra spark plugs is useful when your outboard motor acts up. Another useful aid is a 3-foot length of shock cord. Fastened near your seat, the cord can be used quickly to tie the boat to a stump or limb when anchoring isn't convenient.

Although the list of accessories is as unlimited as your imagination, purchase only those items that you need now. The roster of dealers in Chapter 3 will be able to supply you with catalogs from which to choose.

# Pirogue: Louisiana "Cajun" Boat

Those of you who have visited the bayou country of Louisiana have probably noticed the natives poling a wooden craft which, at first glance, reminded you of a dugout canoe. On second look, however, you saw that the craft was closer akin to a flat-bottom john boat, except that it seemed to pole easier. Then you really got curious. Just what was this mysterious vessel that the late Hank Williams mentioned several times in his hit song, *Jambalaya*. You remember the words: "So, goodbye, Joe...me gotta go...pole the pirogue...down the bayou."

Actually the pirogue is a Cajun work boat. The natives use it daily for trapping, moss gathering, fishing, and hunting. In some cases it is used for travel. There is even a World Championship Pirogue Race, held each May on the picturesque Bayou Barataria, 20 miles south of New Orleans.

This double pointed flat bottom boat has a small draft which makes it ideally suited for fishing, hunting, and exploring shallow waters. It's light in weight, very similar to a canoe, and like most boats of this design, can be loaded and unloaded easily by one person. The pirogue, however, can be tricky to handle, so be sure to wear your life jacket while you're learning to operate it.

The pirogue described in this chapter was designed by Henry Parker of New Orleans. It can be paddled—or like in the song—

poled. Large scale plans may be ordered from Outdoor Sports, P.O. Box 1213, Tuscaloosa, Ala. 35401. Besides the directions for building the pirogue, George Shelton of Outdoor Sports sells plans for several excellent kayak designs, canoes, V-bottom fishing boats, and sailing cruisers. You can obtain a copy of the firm's latest catalog by writing to George.

The following list of materials is to be used as a guide to purchasing materials, but there is plenty of room for substituting materials of similar quantity and quality. You'll find that this is one of the least expensive crafts you've ever tackled...and probably one of the fastest to build!

1 sheet of D.F. plywood 1/4″ × 4′ × 14′
1″ × 2″ (full) × 8′ cedar for ribs
1″ × 8″ × 6′ for seats (cedar or similar)
2″ × 3″ × 36″ cedar for bow stems
7/8″ × 1 1/8″ × 14′ cedar for chines (2 pcs.)
28′ (14′ each) of 1 1/2″ half round
2 lbs. bronze ring shank nails
1/2 lb. hard setting waterproof glue
2 qts. marine paint (color of your choice)

Before ordering the materials, be sure to read Chapter 3—Boatbuilding Lumber and Materials; you may want to substitute, and this chapter will tell you when and how. Of the items on the materials list, the sheet of 1/4″ × 4′ × 14′ plywood is going to be the most difficult to find at your local lumber supply house. Normally, sheets of plywood aren't available in sheets longer than 10 or 12 feet, although larger sizes can be purchased by special order. However, if you can't find a sheet of 1/4-inch plywood of this size, you can splice shorter lengths of plywood by using the scarf-joining method. Such a joint, when carefully made, is stronger than the plywood panel itself, and for boats like the pirogue, it is completely practical.

A scarf joint is made at a ratio of 1:12; that is, the scarfing distance should be the thickness of the plywood multiplied by 12. Thus, on the 1/4-inch-thick plywood panels used for the sides and bottom of our pirogue, the length of the scarf would be 3 inches (Fig. 8-1).

So if you can't find a sheet of 1/4-inch plywood 14 feet long, you can still build the boat using two sheets of conventional

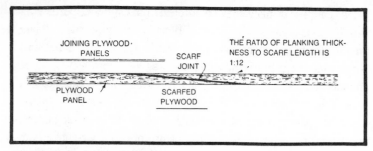

JOINING PLYWOOD
PANELS

THE RATIO OF PLANKING THICK-
NESS TO SCARF LENGTH IS
1:12

SCARF
JOINT

PLYWOOD
PANEL

SCARFED
PLYWOOD

Fig. 8-1. Ratio of planking thickness to scarf length should be 1:12; for 1/4-inch plywood this will be 3 inches.

1/4″ × 4′ × 8′ exterior plywood, A-B grade or better. Begin construction by ripping four pieces of 12″ × 8′ from the two pieces of plywood—two pieces from one sheet and two pieces from the other. Do not attempt to make the splice prior to cutting each piece to the required length because wide panels are very difficult to join properly by the scarf-joining method.

The simplest way to cut the required angle in the two sheets of plywood is to lay one of the 8-foot pieces on a flat surface accessible to a radial arm power saw. Align the second 8-foot piece with the first and let them overlap by 4 inches (see Fig. 8-2). Note that the second piece is supported with scrap material of the same thickness as the first piece. Next align the two panels on the work surface so that they are precisely parallel. Clamp, nail, or screw them down so they won't shift while you're sawing them. Now turn the head on the radial arm saw so that you can make a cut at an angle that'll yield the 3 inches of scarf.

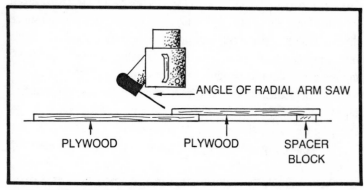

ANGLE OF RADIAL ARM SAW

PLYWOOD          PLYWOOD          SPACER
BLOCK

Fig. 8-2. Method of aligning two pieces of plywood for cut.

After the two pieces have been cut, repeat the same process on the other two pieces—these will be used for the boat siding. When all cuts have been made, coat the joints with a liberal amount of hard setting glue and join them. Again make certain that the pieces to be joined are perfectly aligned before clamping the joint with a wooden block as shown in Fig. 8-3. Note that wax paper is used between the plywood panels and the clamping block, as well as between the panels and the work surface. The wax paper prevents the panels from sticking to the table or the clamping block. To further guard against slipping, nails should be driven through the scarf joint into the work surface. The clamping block should also be secured to the work surface with nails or screws. Nails and screw holes will have to be filled later with fiberglass putty or some similiar material.

When the joint has set in accordance with the time and temperature recommendations of the glue manufacturer, the joint should be as strong as the plywood itself. However, as a safety measure, affix a butt block on the inside of the hull above the scarf joint after the side panels have been installed. You should endeavor to locate these joints where the stress of bends is least.

Take one of the spliced plywood sections (which should now be approximately 12″ × 15′8″) and make a mark at a point 5 1/2 inches in from the bottom end (as shown in Fig. 8-4). Use a straightedge to draw a line from the top outside of the panel to your previously established point and cut as shown in the illustration. From the top of the panel, measure down exactly 14 feet and use a carpenter's square to cut the panel square. Measure in 5 1/2 inches as before

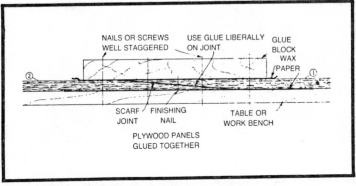

Fig. 8-3. Method of clamping joint with wooden block.

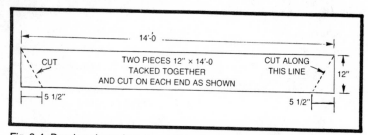

Fig. 8-4. Drawing shows how to cut side planking for pirogue.

and cut the angle as shown in Fig. 8-4. You have just completed one of the side panels for the pirogue. Repeat this operation for the other side panel.

Next take the piece of 2″ × 3″ × 36″ cedar stock and cut out the bow stems according to the full size pattern in Fig. 8-5. Do not detach this pattern from the book. Rather, draw the pattern with transparent tracing paper. Lay the paper on the wood stock and

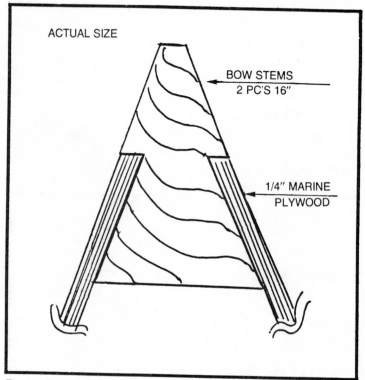

Fig. 8-5. Full size pattern for bow stems.

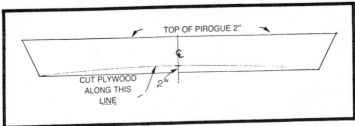

Fig. 8-6. Drawing shows method of trimming side planking to make sides level after planks have been bent into proper position.

transfer the pattern by perforating (at 1/4-inch intervals) the stock with an awl, ice pick, or other sharp pointed utensil. Use a hand saw or backsaw to notch the stock according to the pattern. The 36-inch piece is then cut in half to produce two 18-inch pieces...one for each end of the boat.

In preparation for fastening the sides of the boat to the bow stem, determine the centerline of the side and mark a point along the line two inches from the bottom (Fig. 8-6). Bend a 16-foot length of molding to form a smooth arc between this point and the lower corners of the side panel. Pencil a line along the arc and remove the molding. Align the second side with the first and clamp them together. Then cut both sides at once by rip sawing along the arc.

Figure 8-7 shows the details of jointing the sides to the bow stems. First coat the contacting surfaces with a hard setting glue and then nail as shown in the drawing, using a temporary spacer in the center cut from the piece of 1/2-inch plywood according to the dimensions in Fig. 8-8. You may want to tack this spacer in place with four finishing nails until the permanent rib frame has been installed.

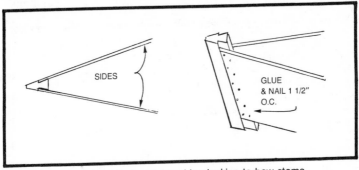

Fig. 8-7. Drawing of details for joining side planking to bow stems.

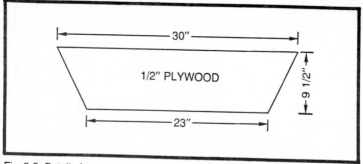

Fig. 8-8. Details for constructing temporary spacer.

While the glue on these joints is setting up, take the piece of 1″ × 2″ (full cut) × 8′ cedar and lay out the center rib frame according to the measurements in Fig. 8-9. Be sure to cut notches for the chines and to glue all joints before nailing. You will also note that a spreader (brace) is tacked in place to hold the frame firm during construction. When the entire boat has been completed, this spreader can be removed.

After the frame is completed and the glue in the side/bow stem joints has set up, extract the four nails holding the temporary spacer. Insert the permanent rib frame and remove the temporary spacer. Make certain the rib frame is centered before gluing and nailing in place. You may become somewhat alarmed at the appearance of the pirogue at this time, as it will be slightly deformed. This is only temporary and your craft will begin to shape up in a short time...so don't be discouraged.

Before you go any further, trim the bow stems by sawing them flush with the plywood sides. You will now work from the bottom of the boat for a while. Bevel both ends of each chine to make them

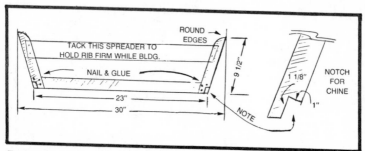

Fig. 8-9. Details for constructing center rib frame.

conform to the stem angles, then fit the chines to the bottom edges of the side panels. Proceed from one stem to the other, using C-clamps to assist the fitting. When one of the chines has been fitted properly, remove it and coat it with glue. Then return it to its permanent position and secure to the bottom with nails at 12-inch intervals. When you're satisfied that the chine has been joined suitably, secure with more nails, this time at 1 1/2-inch intervals. Now go to the other side and fit and install the other chine in the same manner. Remember, though, to allow the chines to project above the sides a quarter-inch or so to allow for trimming and fairing of the bottom.

Continue by planing the projecting edges of the chines all along the bottom. To level the chine edges for receiving the plywood bottom panel, use a straightedge as shown in Fig. 8-10. Continue until the chines will seat flatly against the bottom on each side.

Now turn your attention to the remaining pieces of 1/4-inch plywood. If you were able to obtain a sheet of plywood 14 feet long, then the installation of the bottom will be easy. If you had to settle for two 8-foot pieces of 1/4-inch, then you'll have to make another scarf joint.

Due to the width of the bottom (30 inches at the center), it may not be practical to use a saw when cutting the scarf joint angle. However, a jig or fixture in conjunction with a plane will serve the purpose. First align the two sections of plywood on the edge of a flat

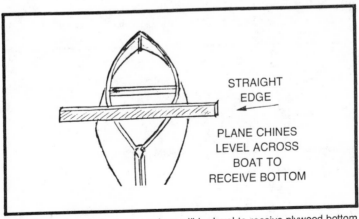

Fig. 8-10. To ensure that chine edges will be level to receive plywood bottom panel, use a straight edge.

179

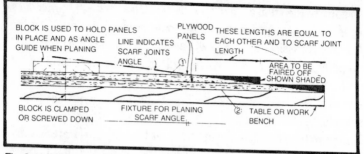

BLOCK IS USED TO HOLD PANELS
IN PLACE AND AS ANGLE
GUIDE WHEN PLANING

LINE INDICATES
SCARF JOINTS
ANGLE

PLYWOOD
PANELS

THESE LENGTHS ARE EQUAL TO
EACH OTHER AND TO SCARF JOINT
LENGTH

①

AREA TO BE
FAIRED OFF
SHOWN SHADED

BLOCK IS CLAMPED
OR SCREWED DOWN

FIXTURE FOR PLANING
SCARF ANGLE

②   TABLE OR WORK
BENCH

Fig. 8-11. Method of aligning two pieces of plywood for planing prior to making scarf joint.

workbench or table—one on top of the other. The upper panel should be set back exactly three inches from the lower panel as shown in Fig. 8-11. Now align the side edges of the two pieces of plywood, the work surface, and the wood block so that they are precisely parallel. Secure the pieces of plywood and the block with clamps or nails so that they cannot move. Then cut the joint with a plane, using the clamping block as an angle guide. The holes made by the nails or other fasteners during this operation must be filled with fiberglass putty or another suitable filler after the panels have been joined.

When the joint has set up according to the glue manufacturer's recommendations, lay the piece of plywood (approximately 2' × 14') on the bottom over top the chines and temporarily tack in place. Scribe along the sides, leaving a 1/4-inch margin all around. Next, apply a hard setting glue to all mating surfaces and insert the plywood bottom in place. Nail the bottom to the chines with one nail

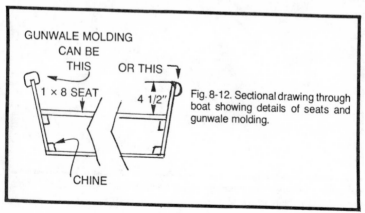

GUNWALE MOLDING
CAN BE
THIS    OR THIS

1 × 8 SEAT

4 1/2"

Fig. 8-12. Sectional drawing through boat showing details of seats and gunwale molding.

CHINE

every foot or so. Then go back and complete the fastening by driving nails every 1 1/2 inches. After dressing the edges of the bottom with a plane and sanding to a smooth finish, you have completed the bottom of your boat.

Turn the boat upright and install the gunwale molding along the top edge of the sides as shown in Fig. 8-12. Use glue and brads to secure the molding. A detail of the molding is shown in Fig. 8-13. Note that the builder has the option of using 1 1/2-inch half round molding (applied to the top outside edge of the sides) or grooved cap molding (slipped over the top edge of the sides). The latter type will give a neater appearance, but it is more difficult to install.

A seat (Fig. 8-12) will be positioned at each end of the craft, approximately 48 iches from the bow stem. The seats will lie 4 1/2 inches blow the gunwales and will rest on 1″ × 2″ wooden cleats fastened to the inner surfaces of the side panels. You may wish to install bow caps and eye bolts as shown in Fig. 8-14.

After all the carpentry work is completed, fill in the holes, gaps, etc., with fiberglass putty or a suitable substitute. Sand all surfaces smooth, and thoroughly clean the entire craft. Apply one coat of primer to all wood surfaces, and then cover with one or two coats of good quality marine paint in the color of your choosing. If the boat is to be used primarily for duck hunting, you might prefer to paint it a

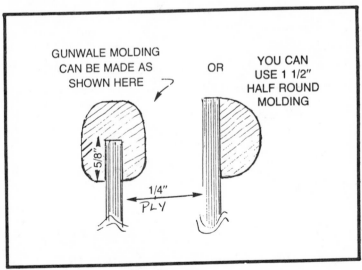

Fig. 8-13. Detail drawing of two types of gunwale molding.

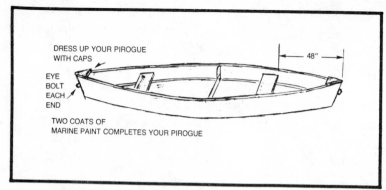

DRESS UP YOUR PIROGUE
WITH CAPS

48"

EYE
BOLT
EACH
END

TWO COATS OF
MARINE PAINT COMPLETES YOUR PIROGUE

Fig. 8-14. Finished boat showing location of seats.

dead grass color or use a camouflage pattern. Some builders favor bright blue and two-tone colors like green and white. The choice is yours, and you can dress up your pirogue as time or fancy permits.

As mentioned previously, a pirogue of this design can be cartopped easily by one adult. Its narrow width also makes it suitable for transporting in a pickup truck or in the back of one of the larger station wagons.

# Build Your Own Canoe

The construction of a canoe is not easy. It is a task that requires weeks of careful and tedious work even for the professional. The amateur, therefore, should not attempt building a canoe—at least not by standard methods—unless he is a very painstaking workman and well experienced in the use of woodworking tools. Yet an amateur *can* build a canoe if he'll address his energies to the simple plywood canoe described in this chapter!

Before getting into the construction details, however, let's take a look at conventional canoes so that you will have a better idea of what you're shooting for. There are five distinct types of canoes used in North America: the all wood design; the canvas canoe; the almost-extinct birch bark canoe; the aluminum canoe; and the fiberglass canoe. All other types are hybrids. The authentic birch bark canoe is only built by certain Indian tribes and by a limited number of non-Indian builders who produce only a few each year. These canoes are extremely hard to obtain and even harder to construct—just like the canvas canoe.

To understand the procedures for building birch bark or canvas canoes, let's briefly study the various steps. This introduction will help you to appreciate the simplicity of the plywood canoe described later.

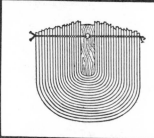

Fig. 9-1. Method of bending and drying ribs for a conventional canoe.

The material for the ribs and lining is perhaps the most critical consideration of the entire construction. These members should be made from cedar, balsam, spruce, or if these woods aren't available, from some other type of light free-bending wood. This lumber should be split, shaved and planed to a thickness of 1/4 to 3/8 inches and a width of 2 inches for the average size canoe. Notice that we said "split." If sawed, these members will not stand the bending required later.

Immediately after each rib is made, it should be placed in water to prevent drying until the time when it will be bent into its finished shape. After enough ribs have been made, they should be placed in a steam box for a few minutes, then removed and bent over a form as shown in Fig. 9-1. Two forms will be required. The ribs will be air dried on the forms for several weeks. Notice that the ribs placed first on the forms (Fig. 9-1) will be of the proper size and shape for the ends of the canoe, while those on the outside of the pack are for the center. In using the ribs after they have dried, the builder works each way from the center. Because this procedure requires two ribs of the same size and shape, two forms will be needed. In other words, the ribs bound on a single form as in Fig. 9-1 are only enough for half of one canoe.

While the ribs are drying, begin work on the lining. The lining is made up of strips about 2 inches wide and 1/8 inch thick for canoes up to 15 feet in length. Cedar is usually the type of wood used. Again, it is best if these strips are split, not sawed. Afterwards, they should be planed to shape. The gunwales which come next should be made of tough wood like white oak. They consist of two pieces and should be shaped as shown in Fig. 9-2. It is best to split these from a tree and shave them down to a 1″ × 1″ size to facilitate bending them

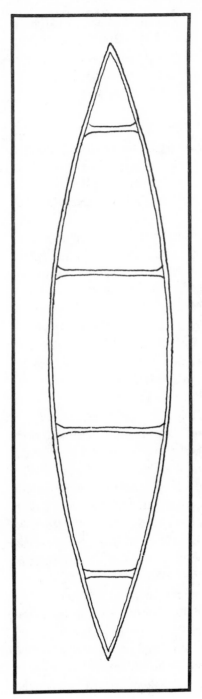

Fig. 9-2. Two pieces of white oak or other tough wood should be shaped as shown here.

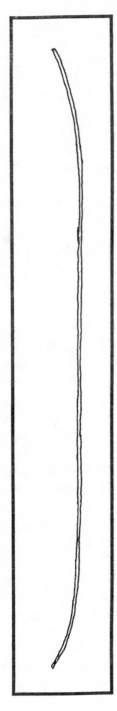

Fig. 9-3. Canoe gunwales steamed and bent in this position and allowed to dry on a form.

around the corners. For a 15-foot canoe the gunwales should be cut 15 feet long, even though the curve (Fig. 9-2) will shorten them somewhat. However, the vertical ends of the canoe also curve and this will return the total length to 15 feet when the craft is completed. The gunwales should be steamed and bent as shown in Fig. 9-3 and allowed to dry on a form.

Refer again to Fig. 9-2 and notice that four crossbars (braces) are used for a 15-foot canoe. These should be mortised into place as shown and fastened with a few small boat nails. The two crossbars closer to the center of the craft should be about 2' 8" long while the outer two—each placed about 2 feet from the ends—should be about 17 inches long.

The strips used for the lining must be fastened together at each end with cord and hung inside the canoe while the ribs are installed. The ribs are then trimmed to the required length, and sprung— starting at the center and working alternately towards either end— under the gunwales. They should be spaced about a half-inch apart. Once the ribs are in place, the lining strips should be fitted together neatly and tacked to the ribs. Before the end ribs are placed in position, however, a narrow half round strip should be stretched and bent to the proper shape and fitted in to cover the seam. A thin narrow strip of wood should then be nailed to the top of the gunwales to protect the edges of the birch bark or canvas body fabric.

If you want to try your hand at covering the canoe with birch bark, it can be done, but good bark has become so scarce that it's almost impossible to find. Check into this before beginning. The Indian method was to sew up the bark with split and boiled spruce or tamarack roots while the bark was still fresh from the tree. Modern materials, however, will make this phase of the construction go easier. Still, at best it's slow work, and in olden times several squaws would work together on the sewing, so that the job could be completed before the bark became too brittle.

All of the bark—including that portion attached to the gunwales—was sewn (not nailed) to the framing and applied to the craft with the flesh side out. To give the canoe the proper shape, two sets of stakes were driven firmly into the ground and the ends of the canoe pinched between the stakes. The ends rested on blocks of wood and the inside was weighted with stones to give curve to the bottom. The seams were then daubed with boiled spruce gum which hardened immediately and made the canoe perfectly waterproof.

If you prefer to go with a more conventional canvas covering over the cedar lining, obtain 12-ounce double-filling duck in one piece and cut it to the shape shown in Fig. 9-4. The canvas should be about 6 feet wide and—to allow for good seams—about 8 inches longer than the canoe. Fasten the canvas to the gunwales on the outside, and tack to the top edge with very small flat headed tacks placed close together. Fasten the ends first, then the center, and finally midway between. The ends of the canvas should then be sewn up with the seams inside.

At no time during the construction of the craft should the canvas be allowed to become wet or even damp and possibly cause shrinkage. Furthermore, wet canvas often won't stretch properly. After the dry canvas has been stretched into place, you're ready for the final steps of oiling and painting the canoe. It is customary to administer liberal applications of hot boiled linseed oil to the canvas. When the canvas has dried thoroughly, paint it with any type of marine paint. Only the canvas, however, should be painted; the bare wood should be primed with a clear wood filler and varnish. Figure 9-5 shows what the finished canoe should look like.

The most primitive type of canoe is the wood dugout which was recorded in ancient history. It is still used today in some South American countries and in other parts of the world. Dugout canoes were built by felling a suitable tree and then chopping and burning it. With the trunk lying on the ground, several workers would carry on the chopping-and-burning procedure until one side of the trunk was slightly flattened. Then they would hollow out the craft with more chopping and burning. These very crude shaping procedures were just about all that the fabrication consisted of.

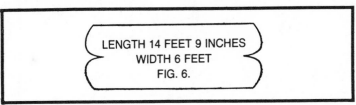

LENGTH 14 FEET 9 INCHES
WIDTH 6 FEET
FIG. 6.

Fig. 9-4. Shape of 12-ounce double-filling duck (canvas) prior to applying to canoe.

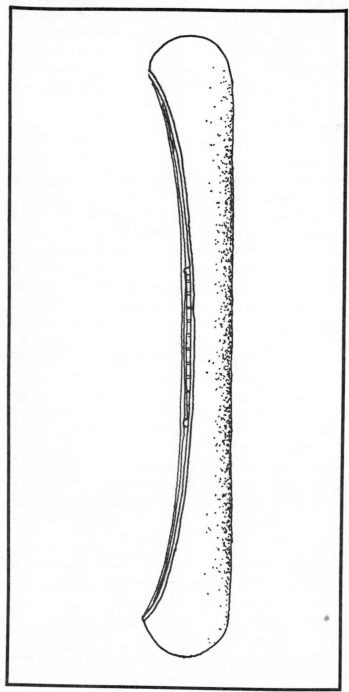

Fig. 9-5. A finished canvas-covered canoe.

Modern wood canoes are constructed of wood planking or laminated sheets molded into shape in the way that fiberglass and aluminum canoes are formed. The type of canoe described later in this chapter for amateur building consists of a combination of wood and fiberglass so that the construction can be accomplished by the first-time boatbuilder.

Unlike the canoes described previously, this design only requires one rib where the others need a dozen or so. Moreover, the ribs don't have to be steamed and bent—they are merely cut from plywood or whole lumber. In place of the cedar skin so difficult to split and plane on classic canoe designs, plywood is used; elsewhere on the craft, fiberglass replaces canvas and birch bark. The result is a canoe that is tough and scrape-proof. Better yet, you can build this canoe in a tenth of the time it would take you to turn out a multi-ribbed conventional canoe.

This craft can be built with a square stern for use with an outboard motor (Fig. 9-6), or as a double-ender (Fig. 9-7) for paddling. Before beginning construction, obtain the following materials:

## MATERIALS LIST

| No. | Size and Description | Use |
|---|---|---|
| | Plywood | |
| 2 pcs | 1/8″ × 4′ × 8′ gum, mahogany or fir | bottom sides |
| 1 pc | 3/4″ × 12″ × 36″ fir exterior AC | center mold |
| 1 pc | 3/8″ × 12″ × 36″ | transom |
| | 1/4″ × 36″ × 60″ | buoyancy seats |
| 1 pc | 3/4″ × 13″ × 15′ | moldings |
| 2 pcs | 3/4″ × 1 1/4″ × 10′ | sheer clamps |
| 1 pc | 3/4″ × 1 1/4″ × 14′ | outer keel |
| 1 pc | 3/4″ × 2 3/4″ × 14′ | inner keel |
| 1 pc | 3/4″ × 5 1/2″ × 8′ | transom frame |
| 1 pc | 3/4″ × 3 1/2″ × 3′ | center brace |
| 1 pc | 1 5/8″ × 9 1/2″ × 12″ | transom keel knee |
| 1 pc | 3/4″ × 7 1/2″ × 24″ | stern, knees, breasthook |
| 1 pc | 3/4″ × 3 1/2″ × 14″ (2 pcs for double ender) | brackets |

Fig. 9-6. Square-stern model designed for use with outboard motor.

190

## Fastenings

1/2 lb   1″ galvanized boat nails
1/4 lb   1″ #18 box nails
1/4 lb   3/4″ box nails
1/2 lb   1 1/4″ galvanized shingle nails
5 doz    1 1/4″ #8 flathead screws
4 doz    2″ #8 flathead screws

## Fiberglass and Cloth

5 yds     50″ wide fiberglass cloth
1 1/2 gal  fiberglass resin with catalyst
12 yds    2″ wide fiberglass tape
1 lb      ground fiberglass fibers

Start construction by making a full size drawing on heavy paper of the planking pattern (Fig. 9-8) that will cover a quarter of the hull. Use a 1/4″ × 3/8″ batten about 8 feet long to draw the curved sheer line and bow lines tangent with the 12-inch radius. Cut out the pattern and place it on a 4′ × 8′ sheet of 1/8-inch plywood as shown in Fig. 9-8. A keel centerline drawn on the plywood will help to locate the pattern. Draw around the pattern to lay out one side, then flip the pattern over and lay out the other side. When cutting the plywood, make a slit the width of the saw blade along the centerline, stopping at a point 48 inches from the bow (as indicated in Fig. 9-8).

If you are going to build the double-ender paddling canoe, lay out and cut another sheet of 1/8-inch plywood as you did the first one. If the square-stern canoe for use with an outboard motor is your choice, do not lay out or cut the second sheet of 1/8-inch plywood. Set these sheets of plywood aside until later and make full size patterns of the parts shown in Figs. 9-9A, B and C. Note that some parts, such as the transom and transom knees, are used only on the outboard-type canoe. Omit these if you build the double-ender. Cut out the patterns and transfer their shapes to plywood or lumber according to the drawings. When fastening the transom frame pieces to the 3/8-inch plywood, coat the contacting surfaces with water-proof glue and use 1-inch galvanized boat nails or 1-inch #6 flat head screws arranged in a staggered double row spaced about 2 inches apart.

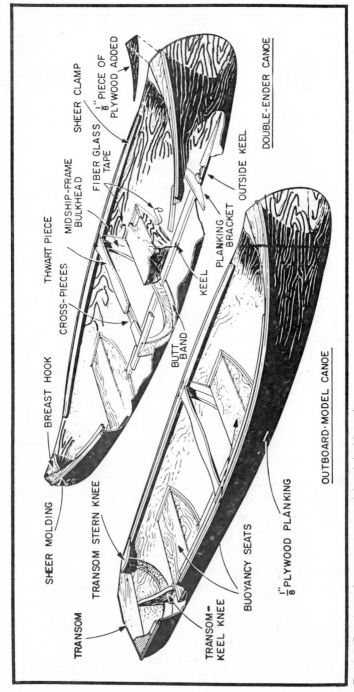

SHEER MOLDING
BREAST HOOK
THWART PIECE
CROSS-PIECES
MIDSHIP-FRAME BULKHEAD
FIBER GLASS TAPE
SHEER CLAMP
$\frac{1}{8}$" PIECE OF PLYWOOD ADDED

DOUBLE-ENDER CANOE

OUTSIDE KEEL
KEEL
PLANKING BRACKET
BUTT BAND

TRANSOM
TRANSOM STERN KNEE
TRANSOM-KEEL KNEE
BUOYANCY SEATS
$\frac{1}{8}$" PLYWOOD PLANKING

OUTBOARD-MODEL CANOE

Fig. 9-7. Drawings of square-stern model and double-ender.

Next, cut the keel (Fig. 9-10) to size and shape. Note that the double-ender keel is tapered at both ends and is somewhat shorter than the keel of the outboard-type canoe. Now, cut a 1/2-inch deep notch in the 3/4-inch plywood midship frame (Fig. 9-11) for the keel. Since two 1/8″ × 6″ plywood pieces—cut from scraps of plywood sheets used for planking—will serve as butt bands to reinforce the seam where fore and aft planking join, cut a notch 6 inches wide and 1/4 inch deep in the keel so the butt band straddles the midship frame (Fig. 9-11).

To assemble the keel and butt bands to the midship frame, first fasten keel to frame with glue and one 1 1/2-inch #8 flat head screw, making sure the frame is square with the keel. Then coat the keel notch and edges of the midship frame with glue and bend one of the 1/8-inch butt bands around the frame (Fig. 9-11), fastening with 1-inch boat nails spaced 3 inches apart. Now coat the contacting

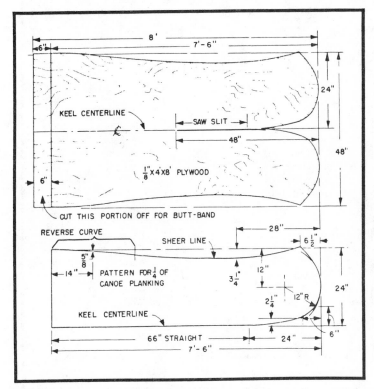

Fig. 9-8. Planking pattern and layout.

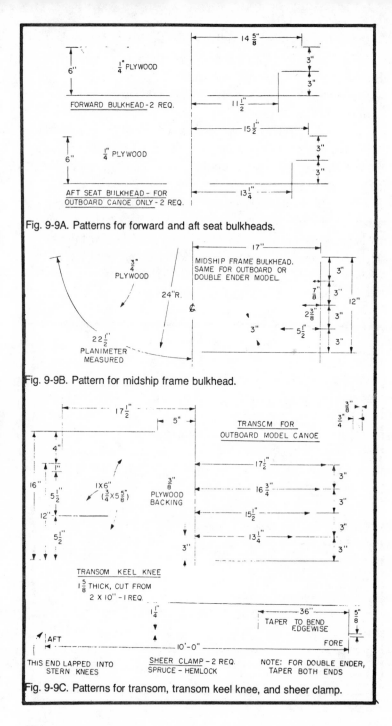

Fig. 9-9A. Patterns for forward and aft seat bulkheads.

Fig. 9-9B. Pattern for midship frame bulkhead.

Fig. 9-9C. Patterns for transom, transom keel knee, and sheer clamp.

194

surfaces of the first and second butt bands and wrap the second band over the first, fastening with 1-inch boat nails as before. Again check to make sure the keel is square with frame and clamp the butt bands to the keel on both sides of the frame until dry.

Next, make a building form consisting of a 2″ × 4″ mounted at a convenient working height on top of legs in the manner of a saw horse as in Figs. 9-10 and 9-12. Cut one planking bracket (Fig. 9-10) if the outboard canoe is to be built—two if the double-ender is your choice—and clamp to a scrap piece of 2″ × 2″ stock mounted 38 inches from the center line. Now place the keel and midship frame assembly in position on the form; mark and cut a notch for the midship frame in the 2″ × 4″ of the building form and clamp in place.

The end of the midship frame can be supported by erecting two 1″ × 2″ braces extending from the floor to the frame ends as shown in Fig. 9-12. Toe nail these supports to the floor and clamp them to the frame. The keel is then lifted up slightly, and the notch in the planking bracket is coated with glue and fastened with one 1 1/2-inch #8 flat head screw. This procedure is followed for both the fore and aft ends of the double-ended canoe. For the square-stern canoe, notch the previously assembled transom to the keel and fasten the transom and transom knee to the keel with glue and three 1 1/2-inch #8 flat head screws at each joint. Be sure the transom is laterally aligned square with the keel. Support is achieved with 1″ × 2″ braces extending to the floor as was done for the midship frame. The bottom surface of the keel is then rounded off with a plane to insure good contact with the plywood skin.

The 1/8-inch plywood skin is bent to shape after it has been steamed or soaked in hot water. The latter process is accomplished by laying rags, burlap, or old rugs on the plywood and saturating the material with hot water. When the plywood is pliable enough to bend, coat the keel, the forward 3 inches of the butt band, and the contacting surfaces of the previously cut plywood planking. Then place the plywood on the frame and position the aft edge at the center of the butt band, thereby making a 3-inch lap. Start shaping the plywood to the frame by bending it around the butt band. Fasten the plywood to the butt band with C-clamps at the sheer ends and bend the bow ends down until the curved ends come together. Tie a rope around the plywood at the bow to hold it in place temporarily.

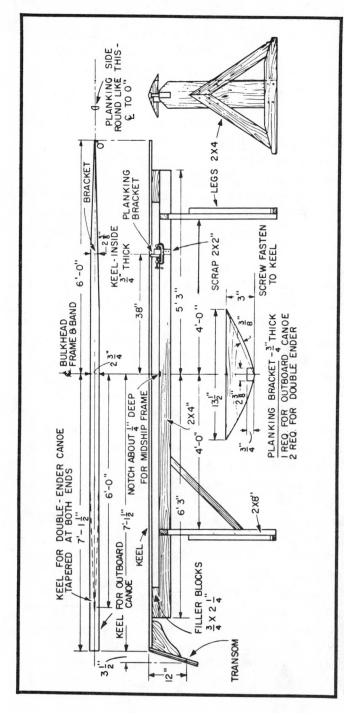

Fig. 9-10. Building framing with dimensions and layout for keel and other attaching members.

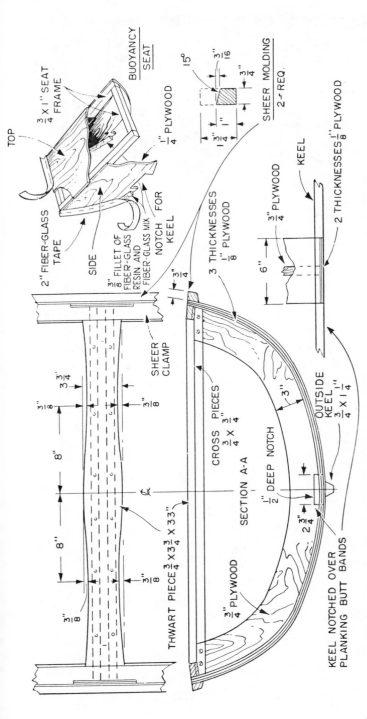

Fig. 9-11. Midship frame and transom are kept in alignment with braces toe-nailed to floor and clamped to frame parts.

197

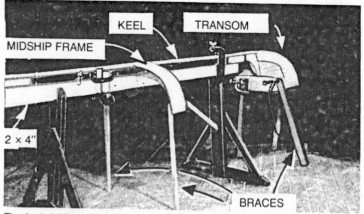

Fig. 9-12. Midship frame and transom are kept in alignment with braces toe-nailed to floor and clamped to frame parts.

Make certain the plywood is accurately centered on the frame and then fasten to the butt band with a staggered double row of 1-inch box nails spaced about 1 1/2 inches apart. Clinch over the nails on the inside. Continue by pulling together the slit-cut edges along the keel and fastening them to the keel with 1-inch nails. Clamp the curved ends together with small C-clamps and fasten with glue and 1-inch nails clinched over. Wooden wedges driven under a steel band (from a packing box) wrapped around the plywood and held together with a C-clamp (Fig. 9-13) will keep the plywood in position until the glue dries.

The aft planking is installed just like the fore planking on the double-ended model. For the square-stern model, however, do not cut the 1/8-inch plywood; rather, soak (as described previously) and wrap the plywood around the transom and butt band. Fasten the plywood to the framing members with glue and 1-inch box nails.

Do not move the hull from the building form for at least 12 hours after the plywood skin is installed—let the glue dry thoroughly. After the glue has dried, remove the clamps and lift the hull from the form. Place it right side up on sawhorses. Fit the breasthook to the pointed end of the canoe as in Fig. 9-7 and secure with glue and 1-inch nails. The double-ender has a similar breasthook at the other end while the outboard canoe design calls for two transom knees at the stern (Figs. 9-14A and 9-14B). Coat the contacting surfaces of the knees with glue and fasten to the transom with two 2-inch #8 flat head screws, and attach to the planking at the sheer line, using 1-inch boat nails.

Rip a 15-foot length of 3/4″ × 1 3/4″ stock as shown in Fig. 9-11 for the sheer molding. Clamp in place on the outside of the planking at the sheer line as in Fig. 9-11 and mark the planking along the molding edges. Remove the moldings, coat the contacting surfaces with glue and reclamp the moldings in place. Fasten the plywood to the moldings with 3/4-inch nails spaced 1 1/2 inches apart.

Make two sheer clamps (Fig. 9-9C) and half lap the ends to fit the transom knees. Notch the clamps to fit over the butt bands, coat all contacting surfaces with glue, and fasten with 2-inch #8 flat head screws spaced 6 inches apart. Then install the two 3/4″ × 3/4″ crosspieces and the thwart piece across the top of the midship frame as in Figs. 9-7 and 9-11.

Now turn the hull over, bottom side up, to install the outside keel. Saw 15° bevels on each side of the keel as in Fig. 9-11 and make the length 13 feet 2 inches for the outboard canoe and 12 feet for the double-ender canoe. Next, taper the end of the keel down to nothing at the bow (Fig. 9-11). Taper both ends for the double-ender. Fasten with glue and 1 1/2-inch #8 flat head screws spaced 6 inches apart. Again turn the canoe right side up so that the buoyancy seats (Fig.

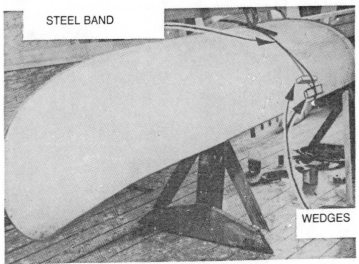

Fig. 9-13. One sheet of 4′ × 8′ plywood planks forward half of the canoe.

199

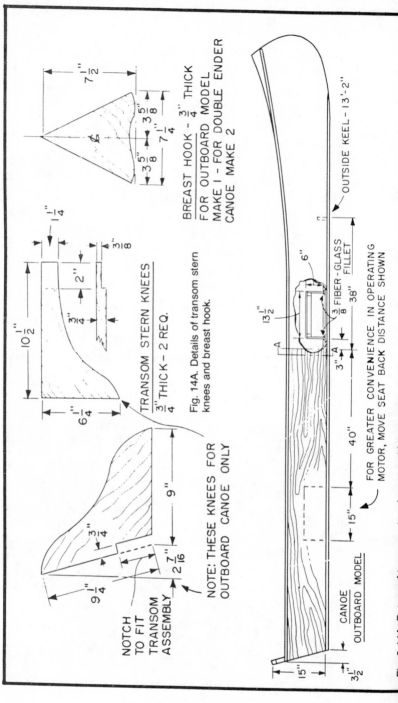

$7\frac{1}{2}''$

$3\frac{5}{8}''$

$3\frac{5}{8}''$   $3\frac{5}{8}''$

$7\frac{1}{4}''$

BREAST HOOK – $\frac{3}{4}''$ THICK
FOR OUTBOARD MODEL
MAKE 1 – FOR DOUBLE ENDER
CANOE MAKE 2

$1\frac{1}{4}''$

$2''$

$\frac{3}{4}''$   $\frac{3}{8}''$

$10\frac{1}{2}''$

$6\frac{1}{4}''$

TRANSOM STERN KNEES
$\frac{3}{4}''$ THICK – 2 REQ.

Fig. 14A. Details of transom stern knees and breast hook.

$9\frac{1}{4}''$

$\frac{3}{4}''$

$9''$

$2\frac{7}{16}''$

NOTCH
TO FIT
TRANSOM
ASSEMBLY

NOTE: THESE KNEES FOR OUTBOARD CANOE ONLY

$13\frac{1}{2}''$

$6''$

$\frac{3}{8}''$ FIBER-GLASS FILLET

$38''$

$3''$

A

A

OUTSIDE KEEL – 13'-2"

$40''$

$15''$

FOR GREATER CONVENIENCE IN OPERATING MOTOR, MOVE SEAT BACK DISTANCE SHOWN

CANOE
OUTBOARD MODEL

$15''$

$3\frac{1}{2}''$

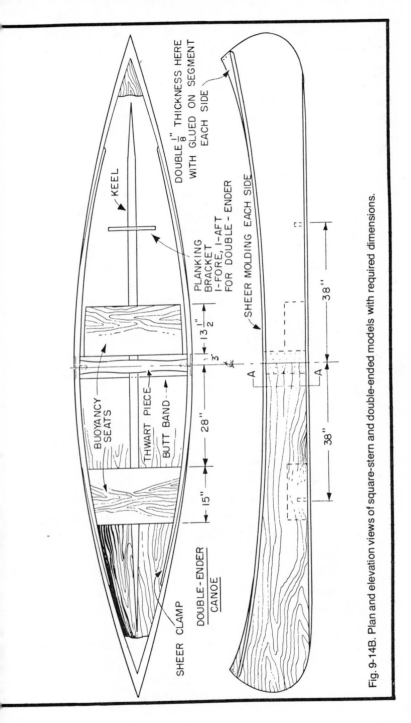

DOUBLE $\frac{1}{8}$" THICKNESS HERE WITH GLUED ON SEGMENT EACH SIDE

KEEL

PLANKING BRACKET 1-FORE, 1-AFT FOR DOUBLE-ENDER

SHEER MOLDING EACH SIDE

BUOYANCY SEATS

THWART PIECE

BUTT BAND

SHEER CLAMP

DOUBLE-ENDER CANOE

$13\frac{1}{2}$"

3"

28"

15"

38"

38"

A

A

Fig. 9-14B. Plan and elevation views of square-stern and double-ended models with required dimensions.

9-7) can be installed. Make cardboard templates of the side pieces shown in Fig. 9-9. Locate the position of these side pieces from the midship frame (Fig. 9-11) and mark the inside of the hull. Since the templates are only an approximation of their shape, fit, mark, and trim each template individually so that it follows the inside contour of the hull. If you cut too much off a template, discard it and make a new one. A good fit is important because these buoyancy seats are actually flotation chambers that will keep the canoe and occupants afloat if capsizing occurs.

After fitting the templates, transfer their outline to 1/4-inch plywood and saw to shape. Make up the 3/4″ × 1″ seat frame and fasten the sides to the frame with glue and nails. Use fiberglass resin to coat the areas inside the hull that will be in contact with the seat sides and frame. Then before the resin dries, place the seat in the hull. Next fasten with three nails driven through the planking into the seat frame on each side. To make a watertight seam where the seat sides meet the hull, make up a heavy paste-like mixture of fiberglass resin and ground glass fibers, and apply a 3/8-inch fillet of the mixture as in Fig. 9-11. Then glue and nail the 1/4-inch plywood top in place and seal all corners and seams with 2-inch fiberglass tape and three coats of fiberglass resin.

Covering the outside of the hull is your next step. First turn the canoe upside down on two sawhorses and prop it up so that one side of the canoe, from sheer to keel, lies as flat as possible. If you are using 50-inch wide fiberglass cloth, cut the cloth down the middle to obtain two 25-inch wide pieces.

Mix about 1 quart of fiberglass resin and apply the substance to the entire side of the canoe, including the outside keel. If uneven absorption leaves dull areas or spots, touch up these with another coat of resin. Now place fiberglass cloth on the hull side so that one long edge is against the bottom of the sheer molding. Mix another quart of resin and apply to the fiberglass cloth, starting along the sheer clamp and working toward the keel, bow and stern. Keep stretching and pressing the cloth gently to remove any wrinkles as you saturate it with the resin. Do not mix more than a quart of the resin at a time because it sets up rather quickly and soon becomes unmanageable. Also have a pan of warm water with household detergent or soap handy to remove the resin from your hands.

When you reach the keel, wrap the cloth over it and trim off the excess cloth. Wrap the cloth around the bow and stern too. Then turn the hull over and apply fiberglass cloth to the other side, again overlapping the keel, bow and stern. Apply three coats of resin and allow each coat to harden before applying the next one. After the last coat has hardened, remove high spots with a disc sander and smooth the surface with fine sand paper.

For color, a pigment can be mixed into the last coat of resin if desired. For those of you who wish to paint your canoe, use two thinned coats of Dolphinite #9585 undercoat on the outside, followed with two thinned coats of deck and ship paint #9007. The inside of the hull will look good with two coats of Dolphinite #9400 rowboat paint. Molding and cross bars should be varnished bright.

Any round bottom canoe with a small, flat shoe keel is ideal for stream and river travel, but it does demand some balancing skill. For family canoeing, one or two outriggers will increase safety and are simply attached. An outrigger can easily be improvised with two lengths of 2″ × 4″ lumber, two innertubes, and four C-clamps. Cut the 2 × 4s into 6-foot lengths; center them across the canoe and clamp to the gunwales. Then stretch an innertube over each end of the 2 × 4s as shown in Fig. 9-15. A pair of simple outriggers like these will make any canoe as stable as a flat bottom john boat.

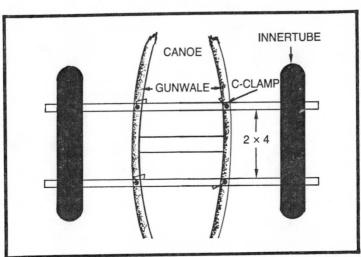

Fig. 9-15. Method of improvising canoe outrigger with 2″ × 4″ lumber, C-clamps, and two innertubes.

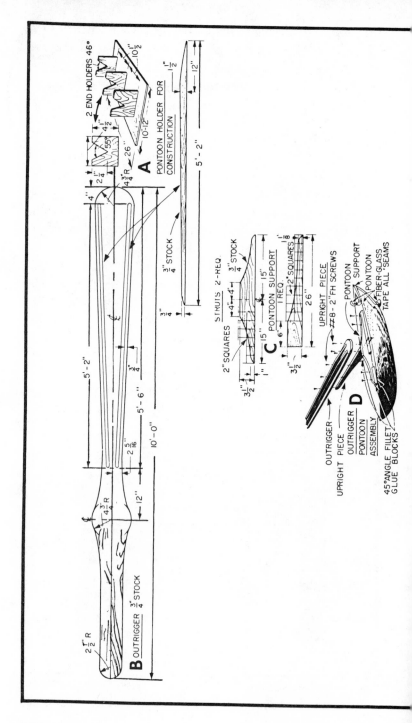

2 END HOLDERS 46°

$1\frac{1}{2}$"

$10\frac{1}{2}$"

$4\frac{1}{2}$"

55°

$2\frac{1}{4}$"

26"

$4\frac{3}{4}$R"

**A** PONTOON HOLDER FOR CONSTRUCTION

10-12'

$\frac{3}{4}$" STOCK

$1\frac{1}{2}$"

12"

5'-2"

$3\frac{1}{4}$"

4"

$4\frac{3}{4}$R

5'-2"

$\frac{3}{4}$

5'-6"

$2\frac{5}{16}$"

10'-0"

$4\frac{3}{4}$R

12"

$2\frac{1}{2}$R

**B** OUTRIGGER $\frac{3}{4}$" STOCK

STRUTS 2-REQ.

$\frac{3}{4}$" STOCK

2" SQUARES

4"  4"

15"

$3\frac{1}{2}$"

1"

**C** PONTOON SUPPORT 1 REQ.

$1\frac{1}{8}$'

2" SQUARES

6"

15"

$3\frac{1}{2}$"

2'6"

UPRIGHT PIECE

1'1"

#8 - 2"FH SCREWS

OUTRIGGER

UPRIGHT PIECE

OUTRIGGER

PONTOON

**D** PONTOON ASSEMBLY

PONTOON SUPPORT

PONTOON

FIBER-GLASS TAPE ALL SEAMS

45°ANGLE FILLET GLUE BLOCKS

204

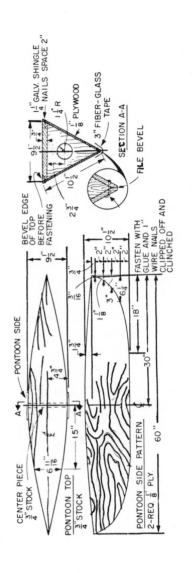

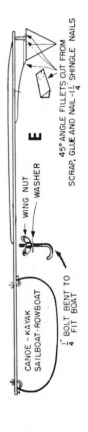

Fig. 9-16. Details for constructing outrigger and pontoon for canoes, kayaks, sailboats, and rowboats.

205

A single outrigger designed especially for the canoe described in this chapter can be built in a couple of hours. While this type is not any safer than the improvised, innertube types, it is somewhat more attractive and you may want to build one.

Figure 9-16 shows how to begin construction of the outrigger by laying out one of the sides on a piece of 1/8-inch plywood. You can obtain the required curve by springing a wooden batten (1/4″ × 1/2″ × 6″) around the dimensions in the drawing. After sawing the first side to shape, use it as a pattern for the second side to insure that both sides are exactly the same.

To determine the exact size of the center piece, make a full size drawing of section A-A in Fig. 9-16 on heavy paper. Transfer the outline of the center piece to 3/4-inch stock and cut to shape. Now, lay out the top (Fig. 9-16) by using a batten sprung against measured points as you did for the sides; then saw to shape.

To aid in assembling the pontoon, make a holder (Fig. 9-16A) from scrap material. When finished, place the two sides in the V-shaped cutouts of the base and insert the center piece between them. Then with a flat file held between the edges of the pontoon sides that are to be joined, file a slight bevel on the edges as in the enlarged detail of section A-A in Fig. 9-16. Since the top piece fits inside the pontoon side pieces, the edges of the top will have to beveled. To do this, temporarily clamp the edges of the sides together, place the pontoon top piece in position and mark for beveling. Plane and fit the top piece so that the beveled edges will make wood-to-wood contact with the sides.

Start assembling by fastening the center piece to the center of the underside of the top with four 1 1/2-inch #8 flat head screws. Coat all joining surfaces of the sides, center piece, and top with a thick mixture of waterproof glue and fasten the sides to the top with 1 1/4-inch galvanized shingle nails spaced about 2 inches apart. Then clamp the edges of the sides together (Fig. 9-17) and fasten with 1-inch box nails driven through both sides as in Fig. 9-16. Clip off the projecting ends of the nails to within 1/8 inch of the sides and clinch by holding an iron on the nailhead side and bend by pounding over the nail on the other side. After the glue dries, trim all edges evenly and sand smooth, taking care to round the edges of all corners.

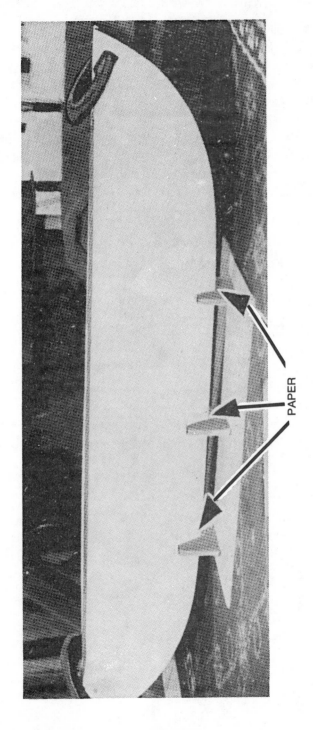

PAPER

Fig. 9-17. Place pieces of paper between hull and holder at bottom of V-blocks to prevent hull from becoming glued to holder.

207

Make the pontoon outrigger, upright, and support (Figs. 9-16B and 9-16C) and fasten to the pontoon with glue and 2-inch #8 flat head screws. Reinforce with 3/4-inch triangular glue blocks glued and nailed to the support, upright, and pontoon top as in Fig. 9-16D.

To make the pontoon watertight, first cover the entire pontoon with one coat of fiberglass resin and then apply 2-inch wide fiberglass tape to all pontoon seams and saturate the tape with resin. After the resin has hardened, sand smooth and finish with two coats of enamel undercoater followed with two coats of marine enamel of the desired color. After the outrigger has been painted, fasten it to the canoe with two 1/4-inch bolts bent to a J-shape as shown in Fig. 9-16E.

## MATERIALS LIST FOR OUTRIGGER AND PONTOON

| No. | Size and Description | Use |
|---|---|---|
| 1 | 1/8″ × 4′ × 6′ exterior plywood or hardboard | planking |
| 1 | 3/4″ × 9 1/2″ × 72″ spruce or hemlock | top and center piece |
| 6 yds | 2″ fiberglass tape | hull seams |
| 1 pt | fiberglass resin | |
| 1 | 3/4″ × 10″ × 10′ spruce or hemlock | outrigger |
| 1 lb | 1 1/4″ galvanized shingle nails | upright and supports |
| 4 | 1 1/2″ #8 flat head screws | |
| 12 | 1 3/4″ #8 flat head screws | |
| 24 | 2″ #8 flat head screws | |
| 1 lb | glue (Weldwood or Elmer's Waterproof) | |
| 2 | 1/4″ × 5″ bolts with wing nuts and washers | |

Large scale drawing for this canoe may be obtained from Craft Prints, 229 Park Avenue South, New York, N.Y. 10003. Ask for Print #266; Price: $6.00.

# Repair and
# Maintenance of Your Boat

While it is true that a fiberglass craft normally requires less maintenance than a wooden craft, all boats still need care and maintenance; so just because you think you have a maintenance-free craft, you can't let her go for long without at least a little care...the no-maintenance claims of some dealers haven't quite panned out.

Generally speaking, the care and maintenance of boats fall into two categories: appearance and operation. The appearance category includes preserving, anti-fouling, and general overall appearance. The operation category involves proper functioning of the hull, motor, controls, lights, trailer, and other necessary accessories.

Getting back to fiberglass boats, when this material was introduced, it was claimed to be maintenance-free...it would never need paint or maintenance. However, after a few years of normal docking, beaching, and trailering, these same boats began to look a bit the worse for wear. Colors faded and the hulls started to show gouges, cracks, and crazing. Happily, all of these can be repaired with ease and the hull itself can be freshened up by using one of the new surface coatings. Here's some practical advice on how to care for your boat—canoe, kayak, or whatever—so that you can obtain the best and longest use of it.

Begin your care and maintenance by giving your boat a bath from time to time. Remove the drain plug (if your craft has one) and hose the entire craft down—both inside and out. Make sure you have removed cushions and other items that should not become wet. After several minutes of hosing, wipe your craft dry with a chamois cloth and clean all hardware with metal polish. After polishing, spray-coat each item with silicone corrosion inhibitor which will keep your hardware showroom-fresh. The upholstery may be cleaned with any of the good vinyl cleaners, but be sure to change rags often because they soil quickly and a dirty rag won't do the job properly.

If the fiberglass boat is three or more years old, more than likely time has taken its toll by fading the color and stealing the sheen of the hull. If this is the case, repaint your fiberglass hull with one of the several surface coatings designed especially for fiberglass. Properly applied these coatings will last three years if you don't bang your boat around too much. Wooden boats that get hard usage, on the other hand, will look best if they are repainted every year since the swelling and shrinking of wood will not permit the paint to last as long as on a fiberglass boat.

Dents and cracks in the hull may be repaired with fiberglass kits consisting of resin, hardener, and fiberglass cloth or tape. The use of these kits is fully explained in Chapter 11. Wooden boats with leaking seams may also be repaired with fiberglass tape. First fill all dents and gaps with a good fiberglass putty, allow to dry, and apply fiberglass tape (of the proper width) along the seams. This is done by first coating the area with resin mixed with the correct amount of hardening agent for the ambient temperature. Then apply the tape and smooth out all creases and air bubbles before administering two more coats of resin. Let the first coat dry before putting on the second. You may want to sand lightly between coats to secure a smoother finish.

You can also improve the appearance of your craft by using a one-step car wax; that is, one that contains both a cutting agent and finishing wax in one compound. Most of these compounds wipe dry and are easy to use. However, if your boat surface is really in bad shape as far as oxidizing is concerned, you can use an electric drill adapted with a wool buffing pad to aid you in your polishing. Your boat trailer should be treated every so often—depending upon how often you use your boat—with a similar compound.

Canvas-covered wooden boats—typical of many canoes and kayaks—are relatively simple and inexpensive to maintain and repair. For example, after a season's use on your favorite lake or stream, usually only a light sanding of the craft's interior and one coat of spar varnish will be required to keep it in good shape. On alternate years the interior wood should be well sanded down and given two coats of spar varnish—with light sanding between coats. Also apply one coat of canoe enamel and two coats of high-grade varnish.

If the surfaces (either inside or outside) are in really poor condition, it may be best to completely remove the entire finish with a liquid paint remover. However, if this is done on the outside of a canvas-covered canoe, the paint remover will also remove a portion of the filler on the canvas. Therefore, a new canvas filler must be applied. This may be five coats of wing dope (lightly sanded between coats) or one of the prepared canvas fillers. The wing dope, which is nitrate cellulose, will dry in less than an hour and will shrink the canvas to a snug fit, but it is normally not used if the canvas is glued to the planking. After the filler has completely dried, apply three coats of canoe enamel and two coats of spar varnish. You will then have a practically new canoe.

It is not unusual for the canvas-covered canoe to become damaged on rocks and snags when used on rivers and streams. When such a break in the canvas occurred in the North woods, the canoes were usually repaired on the spot by melting spruce gum in a pot and smearing the viscous substance over the damaged place. The gum hardened immediately and the wound was healed. On large breaks a piece of canvas was used in conjunction with the spruce gum to patch the damaged spot. Time may cause these patched areas to leak, but they can again be made leakproof by running over the seam with a hot iron.

Spruce gum is not readily available to the modern canoeist so small holes are normally repaired by simply filling with marine glue from the outside of the crack. Small rips in the canvas are usually repaired by inserting a patch of light canvas on the inside of the crack—between the planking and the original canvas—and then after flattening out the patch, the entire area is saturated with marine glue. However, before the glue has completely hardened, the area should be neatly smoothed out with a flat iron.

Certain wooden members of a canoe that become damaged or broken can usually be repaired by splicing a new member in place. This group will include the gunwales, ribs, planking, and stem members; although with stem members it is best to replace the entire member.

When it comes to a canvas canoe's covering, the stems or ends are the sections that sustain damage most often. Many owners of canvas-covered canoes, therefore, fiberglass the ends of their craft, back about 18 to 24 inches for added protection. This may be done by using techniques described in Chapter 11. However, your uses of the canoe may not require this, so it is recommended that the fiberglassing not be done until a major repair becomes necessary.

The operational aspects of boat maintenance and repairs include a thorough investigation of all working parts of the craft—and also your boat trailer. The following items deserve special attention: lights (on both boat and trailer), fire extinguisher, life preservers, dock lines, anchor lines, engine, sailing rig, and controls. Many people will overlook the controls—like the steering, throttle, and shift—if they worked well during the season. But at today's high speeds, can you imagine what would happen if you were ripping along at, say, 40 knots, and your steering cable broke? Be suspicious of such things and look around a bit.

The often-neglected trailer should be checked at least yearly for bad bearings, brakes, and hitch-and-tilt mechanism. Just as with your boat, it wouldn't hurt to scrape off the rust and give these areas a touch of matching paint. If the paint is in fairly good shape, you may just want to wash and wax it. This will do wonders in preserving your rig and you will take pride in its sharp appearance.

When repainting your boat or canoe—either fiberglass, wood, or canvas—give the entire surface a light sanding to dull the finish and to give the new coat a surface to which it can bond. Cracks and deep scratches may be filled with fiberglass putty and then sanded flush with adjacent surfaces prior to painting, but be sure you allow enough time for the area to dry before applying the paint.

If you are lucky enough to own a boat with a galley or built-in fresh water tank, be certain to drain the tank at least once in midseason. Add a box of baking soda and fill the tank about 1/8 full of water. Let this mixture slosh around for a few hours—either while rocking during normal operation of the boat or else on the trailer while taking the boat to and from the docks.

Inspect the gas tanks frequently and give special attention to all seams and rust spots. If a rust spot is detected, sand off the rust and repaint after first priming with a rust-inhibitor. However, if the rusting is significant, discard the tank and purchase a new one; a leaking gas tank can be worse than a bomb and may be one of the reasons for the mysterious disappearance of several vessels in the Bermuda Triangle over the years.

Your outboard and inboard motors will need some attention also. Here are a few of the things that are suggested for proper maintenance of either.

1. Clean and de-gum all fuel passages between the gas tank and the carburetor. This of course includes all hoses, filters, fuel pumps, etc. Keep in mind that the gas lines must be airtight throughout, so they should be checked for leaks as well as for worn gaskets before the system begins to suck air.
2. Check seasonally the gasket and diaphragm on the fuel pump; but in any event, replace every third year.
3. Clean and check all filters. Give special attention to gaskets.
4. Check operation of automatic choke.
5. Clean, and reset or replace points.
6. Test condenser and coil. Replace if necessary.
7. Check water pump. Replace impeller often if boat is operated in sandy or muddy waters.
8. Flush out gear case and replace lubricant each year.
9. Inspect propeller. Repair or replace as needed.
10. Check all nuts, bolts, and other fasteners. Tighten if necessary.

You'll also want to check, clean and recharge your battery and examine the rest of your boat's electrical system. Look for cracked insulation, corrosion or other problems which could leak or short-circuit electric current. Inspect the wiring of your boat trailer also; check brakes, lights, etc., and repair if necessary. That traffic ticket away from home could ruin an entire day and cast a pall on your whole vacation.

While you're giving your boat and trailer the once-over, don't neglect your many accessories like the electronic depth sounder, anchors, horns, instrument panel, flares, and the like. All of these have a function to perform on your boat or you wouldn't have purchased them, so make certain all of them work. While we're talking about anchors, have you checked the anchor lines recently? If the lines are made from natural fibers like manila hemp, they will tend to rot unseen on the inside. The next time you lower your anchor overboard may be the last time you see it! Many sailors are now adopting the more practical nylon rope for virtually all lines aboard. Nylon rope has some excellent qualities and it won't rot, but you'd still be wise to check it from time to time.

The old saying, "A stitch in time...." is certainly true when it comes to boat maintenance. A little love and care for your favorite craft will pay off in dividends—more time enjoying yourself on the water and less time effecting repairs in drydock.

# Overhaul Your
# Boat or Canoe with Fiberglass

The introduction of fiberglass a few decades ago brought an entirely new concept to the field of boat building, covering and repairing. This material is reasonable in price and simple to work with. Even a beginner can use it to cover or repair any type of craft. As a covering fiberglass is known for its:

1. Ease of maintenance
2. Neat appearance
3. Durability
4. Light weight
5. High strength
6. Low cost

A properly installed fiberglass boat covering will not leak, waterlog, rot, mildew, rust, or corrode; it is wormproof, weather-proof and gasoline-, oil- and alcohol-proof. Few conditions—like salt water, strong sunlight, or freezing temperatures—will harm fiberglass and it further gives nearly complete protection from barnacles and other marine growth. Here briefly is how fiberglass fibers are made.

Clear glass marbles—like the ones we used to play with at school—are dropped into a stoker above a platinum floored oven (see Fig. 11-1). The oven melts the marbles and the glass liquid is

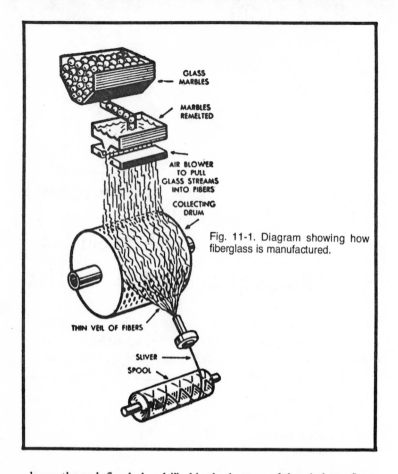

GLASS MARBLES

MARBLES REMELTED

AIR BLOWER TO PULL GLASS STREAMS INTO FIBERS

COLLECTING DRUM

Fig. 11-1. Diagram showing how fiberglass is manufactured.

THIN VEIL OF FIBERS

SLIVER

SPOOL

drawn through fine holes drilled in the bottom of the platinum floor. This precious metal is used because of its ability to withstand high temperatures and because the tiny holes drilled in it do not clog up with molten glass. The filaments formed by this drawing process are as fine and transparent as spider webs. These fibers of glass are then routed over a motor-driven collecting drum (or bobbin) located beneath or adjacent to the oven and at the same time are sprayed with ordinary starch. The starch acts as a binder and makes the fibers visible. The first process is completed when the fibers are spun into yarn and wound onto a spool as shown in the illustration. These spools are then baked at high temperatures (high enough to bake out the starch) and woven into fiberglass cloth, tape, and other forms.

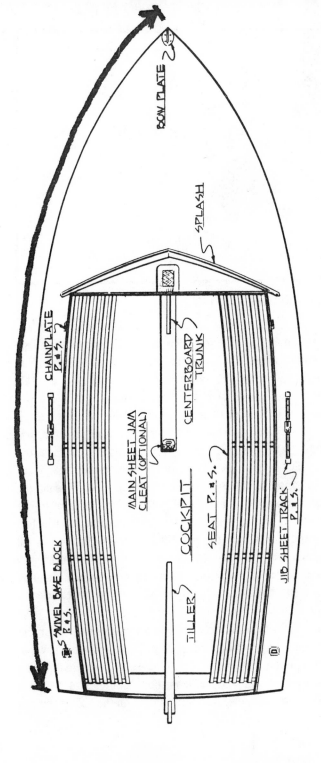

Fig. 11-2. Method of measuring length of boat to obtain total yardage of fiberglass cloth needed.

217

Fig. 11-3. Method of measuring width of boat to obtain size of fiberglass cloth.

## PREPARING FOR FIBERGLASSING

If you plan to fiberglass your entire boat hull, you'll first have to determine the materials that you will need. To find the total yardage of fiberglass cloth needed, measure the length of your boat from bow to stern along the gunwale as shown in Fig. 11-2. Add approximately 12 inches for overlap and then multiply the total length by 2 if you plan to use two pieces of cloth on the bottom of the hull. However, if you use a size of cloth wide enough to cover the whole bottom, you don't multiply by two; just use the linear measurement and add a foot for overlap. Since most fiberglass cloth is sold by the linear yard, your final measurement should reflect the total yardage required.

Measure from the keel or center of the boat bottom to the gunwale at the widest point of your boat. Add approximately 6 inches for overlap and you will have the width of fiberglass cloth that you will need—if you're using two pieces. If you plan to order cloth of a width large enough to cover the bottom of the hull in one piece, multiply your first measurement by 2. Figure 11-3 shows how to measure the width of your boat.

You'll now have to figure a little extra in order to cover the transom or back of your boat; certain john boats may also have an added section in the front of the boat...so be sure to figure on these also. Measure the width and depth as shown in Fig. 11-4. You can add additional cloth of the same width as used on the hull or you can order a separate piece to cover the entire transom at once. You may even have enough material left over from the hull to fiberglass the transom. Just use the scraps—overlapping every edge—and sand the surfaces flush when the fiberglass resinote has hardened...no one will know they are scraps.

One gallon of resinote will be sufficient to cover 140 square feet with one coat. However, you will need a minimum of three coats, so count on about 46 square feet per gallon. This is equivalent to:

| 38"wide | 44"wide | 50"wide | 60"wide |
|---------|---------|---------|---------|
| 5 yds | 4.3 yds | 3.8 yds | 3.16 yds |

## PRACTICAL APPLICATION OF FIBERGLASS

To cover a canoe or similar craft with fiberglass, use heavyweight fiberglass cloth to replace the canvas covering. The ends of canvas canoes usually become damaged before the rest of the craft. If you don't care to cover the entire craft, remove the canvas from the ends only as far back as necessary, and then cover the exposed area with fiberglass cloth and resinote—using methods described later in this chapter. Any type of wooden boat can be covered with heavyweight fiberglass cloth.

While fiberglass is normally used only on the bottom of the hull, it may also be used to cover decks. Use only one layer of heavyweight fiberglass cloth. To produce a non-slipping surface, merely apply an additional coat of resinote, and wait until it becomes tacky; then sprinkle fine sand on the surface with a salt shaker.

To cover hulls longer than 25 feet, use two layers of heavyweight fiberglass cloth instead of one. If you want to build the entire hull from fiberglass, use one layer of fiberglass mat between two layers of heavyweight fiberglass cloth for boats up to and

Fig. 11-4. Method used to measure width and depth of transom to determine amount of fiberglass cloth needed.

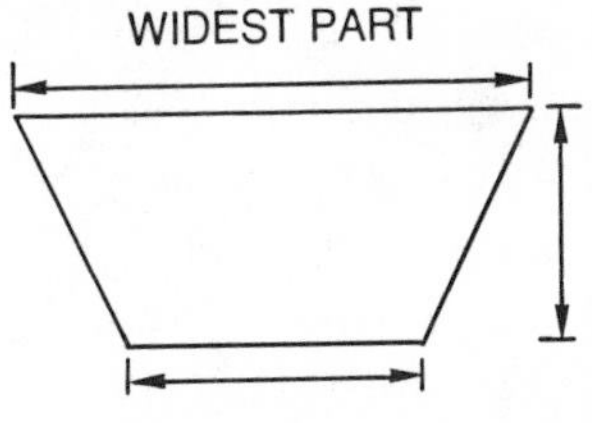

WIDEST PART

including 16 feet. For boats from 18 to 25 feet, an additional fiberglass mat will be required between the two layers of cloth. As described in Chapter 5, a wooden mold is first made, and then the fiberglass material is applied over the mold to form an all-fiberglass hull. When building cruiser hulls, however, additional bottom layers of fiberglass cloth may be required—depending upon the structure of the shell.

If you like the appearance of wood grain, yet want an extra strong and maintenance-free hull, a single layer of fiberglass cloth topped by a coat of clear resinote would be transparent enough to let the grain show through. The fiberglass covering should keep the hull from fouling in almost any waters—like those semi-tropical waters off Florida and Louisiana where marine growth is so abundant.

## BASIC FIBERGLASS PROCEDURES

The preparation of the hull is an important step in acquiring a good fiberglass finish. The fiberglass laminations will not adhere unless all of the old paint has been removed and the hull is perfectly dry. All cracks, dents, etc., should be filled flush to the adjacent surfaces with fiberglass putty or a similar agent and sanded smooth.

It is usually best to have the fiberglass cloth roughly cut to shape before applying any resin to the boat surfaces. Use a pair of old scissors for the cutting, and make certain that the cloth is laid smoothly and that it follows the hull contours in all sections.

At this point, you have two choices: paint the hull with the resin and then lay the fiberglass cloth over it, or place the rough-cut cloth in position and secure with a staple gun before applying the resin. Each method has its advantages and disadvantages, but most people prefer to apply the resin first and then place the cloth.

Mix only one quart of resin at a time; apply the correct amount of hardener for the ambient temperature and the desired drying time. Always follow the manufacturer's instructions to the letter. Now, without delay, use a mohair paint roller or a 3-inch brush and give the bottom of the hull a coat of the resin. If the bottom is to consist of two pieces of fiberglass cloth, only coat one piece at a time. Use the keel as the dividing line and overlap this line 4 or 5 inches. Quickly inspect the surface of the wood for any areas that apear dull. Dull spots occur where the wood has deeply absorbed the resin; they should be coated again immediately.

Now working in the shade and without delay, take your rough-cut piece of fiberglass cloth and—proceeding from one end of the boat—lay the cloth onto the wet resin covering the bottom of the hull (only half of the bottom if two pieces are to be used). Wear rubber gloves to protect your hands, and then press and smooth the cloth with a roller as you lay it on the hull. Work from the keel to the gunwale. An ordinary squeegee can be very helpful during this operation to shape the cloth to the contour of the keel. It would also be helpful to cover a lap strake boat.

One word of caution. It is of the utmost importance that there be *no* air bubbles under the surface of the cloth. Work these out with your roller or hands. In most cases, your finger tips—protected by rubber gloves—are the best utensil for this step. If all fails and you simply cannot dispel one or two of the air bubbles, make a slit or two in the cloth at this point with an old pair of scissors. Then press the cloth back down.

If the hull bottom was to be done in two operations, give the opposite side of the boat a coat of resin, apply the cloth, and smooth out all bubbles as previously described.

Now that the bottom of the hull has been completely covered, give the transom a coat of resin and cover with a piece of rough-cut fiberglass cloth. Overlap the cloth from the transom around the sides of the boat 2 to 6 inches. Cut and fold to fit when necessary to achieve a smooth finish. Again, be absolutely certain to roll out all air bubbles.

When the resin is completely hard, feather sand the overlapping edges so they blend in with the fiberglass covering of the hull. Clean the surface, and apply another coat of resin to the entire hull and transom. Smooth out any bubbles and let the resin cure for several hours.

At this point you're going to have a lot of rough edges around the gunwales, so trim these off with a hacksaw or sabre saw using a fine tooth blade. If you allow the resin to dry until it is barely dry to the touch, but not completely hard, you'll find that the edges extending over the gunwales can be trimmed easily with a sharp utility knife and a sawing motion toward the center of the boat. Apply pressure on the forward stroke—whether with a knife or saw. Pressure on the back stroke will tend to pull loose the fabric.

With the second coat of resin hardened throughout, carefully check the entire surface for pinholes. If any are located, lightly sand and allow them to fill up with the dust of the abrasion. Then use fine sand paper to remove small rough spots and uneven areas. You're now ready for the final coat of resin.

Mix another quart of resin with the correct amount of hardening agent, and apply a third coat to the hull. Since this is the final coat (hopefully), the utmost care should be taken to have this coat very smooth and uniform. If you're using a coloring agent in the resin, mix at one time all the resin and color that you will need for the entire hull. This will insure an even hue all over.

It is not possible to give the exact curing time for all applications since this will vary according to the weather conditions, the temperature, etc. For example, in cold or humid weather, the resin may not become completely hard for perhaps a day or two. In hot and dry weather, it may become hard before you can complete the application. While it is usually best to perform the fiberglass application in the shade, you can shorten the hardening time by moving your boat into the sun once the resin has been applied.

The illustrations in Figs. 11-5 through 11-13 give you a pictorial summary of the preceding instructions. Study them and read the captions every time you begin to work with fiberglass...they'll save you much time and prevent you from omitting any of the steps.

While your boat is curing, think about cleaning up the tools you've been using. Once the resin has hardened, you'll never be able to remove it from rollers, brushes, and the like; so work quickly on the cleaning. Herter's, Inc., of Waseca, Minn., sells a very good fiberglass resin solvent. It is excellent for cleaning rollers, brushes, and your hands. Acetone and lacquer thinners will clean brushes to some extend, but are not nearly as effective as the fiberglass resin custom solvents. Herter's sells fiberglassing materials of all kinds ...at reasonable prices. Materials can also be purchased from your local Sears, Roebuck and Montgomery Ward stores.

## OTHER USES OF FIBERGLASS FOR BOATBUILDING

Ground fiberglass fibers are available for mixing with resin to form a putty-like paste for filling in dents, cracks, and open seams. Once hardened, a fiberglass repair will outlast the original material.

Fig. 11-5. Preparing the hull's surface.

Fig. 11-6. Roughly cut fiberglass cloth to fit general hull shape.

Fig. 11-7. Apply coat of resin to half the boat.

Fig. 11-8. Applying the fiberglass cloth.

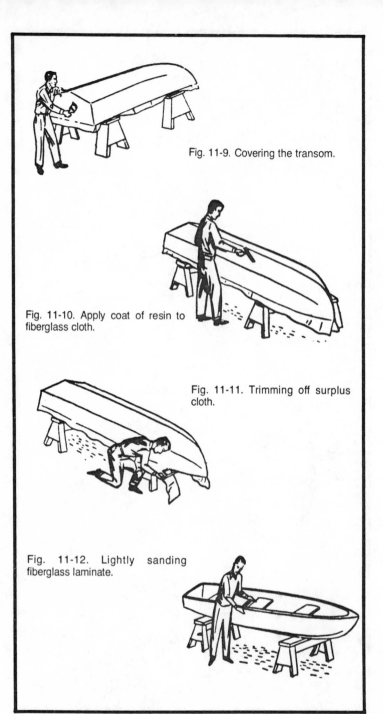

Fig. 11-9. Covering the transom.

Fig. 11-10. Apply coat of resin to fiberglass cloth.

Fig. 11-11. Trimming off surplus cloth.

Fig. 11-12. Lightly sanding fiberglass laminate.

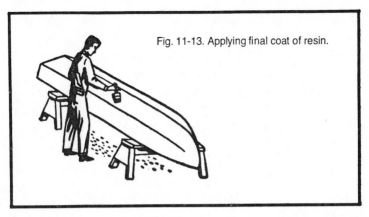

Fig. 11-13. Applying final coat of resin.

If you're mainly concerned with repairing your boat—like perhaps waterproofing some seams which have become loose—then fiberglass tape may be your answer. Some people merely cut strips from regular fiberglass cloth for these repairs, but the resulting raw edges quickly unravel and the effort goes for nought. Special fiberglass tapes are manufactured for the express purpose of repairing and waterproofing boat seams. These tapes are woven individually on looms and their edges are intertwined so they won't unravel. They are suited for any work where a narrow strip of fiberglass is of advantage. Some of the tape's many uses are for:

1. Covering and reinforcing keels and spray rails.
2. Covering boat gunwales.
3. Covering the top of boat transoms.
4. Reinforcing sail boat masts and centerboard edges as well as fishing boat outriggers.
5. Covering oars and paddles.
6. Covering all seams in plywood boats.
7. Covering hard-to-wrap circular objects.

Fiberglass tapes come in sizes from 1 1/2 inches to 6 inches and wider and are applied just like the fiberglass cloth. Clean the surfaces where the tape is to be applied; fill in all cracks, dents, etc., with fiberglass putty. Mix the resin with the correct amount of hardening agent, administer one coat to the area, and apply the tape. Sand lightly and repeat two times.

Fiberglass repair kits are available on the market for less than $5 and work wonders on modern boat and canoe repairs. Regardless of the kind of hole or stoving in your craft, you can quickly and premanently repair it with one of these kits. If the repair work is done on a canvas covered canoe, for example, while on a camping trip, there is really no need to repair the wood at the time. A fiberglass patch over the hole or broken-in part will be several times stronger than the original wood. The wood planking under the patch can be repaired after you return home. These kits are also handy for repairing troublesome boat seams that somehow won't stay sealed during your outings.

Kits like the ones just described are ideal for keeping in the trunk of the car, in your vacation cabin, or stowed away on your boat, since they pack into a very small space and are always ready for instant use. There is no need for special trips to town to obtain repair materials. A typical kit consists of a pint of resin (with hardening agent), 3 or 4 square feet of fiberglass cloth, 6 to 10 feet of fiberglass tape, a small amount of resin solvent, and complete instructions.

Don't feel like you're wasting money when you purchase one of these kits and then don't use it for boat repairs, there will be dozens of other uses for it. No active outdoorsman should be without one...no homeowner either! The kit may be used to repair camping equipment (like closing a hole in your ice cooler); to mend handles on garden tools; to recondition rusted out gutters and downspouts; to renovate damaged trailer and camper bodies—there are dozens of uses for this kit. You can even buy flexible "on-the-spot" fiberglass patches for repairing wood, metal, or fiberglass. Just peel off the backing and apply these 4″ × 6″ patches to the surface; that's all there is to it!

You'll also be interested to know that you can give your boat a permanent paint job at the same time you're applying the fiberglass. Just add coloring pigments to the resin prior to mixing with the hardening agent, and you'll have a paint job that is blended forever into the fiberglass laminate. Adding pigments to resin is much less expensive than painting in the conventional way. Furthermore, a full spectrum of colors is available...every color from white to black.

# Appendix
# Useful Boatbuilding Data

The information contained in this section will prove useful to all concerned with boatbuilding—either for repairs or for the construction of an entire craft.

## ESTIMATING COST OF BOATS

Unlike the purchasing of a new factory-built boat—where an exact price can be obtained from the dealer—those who undertake a boatbuilding project seldom know the exact cost of the boat until the final coat of paint is applied. In some cases, the builder has to give up on the project—or at least delay the construction—due to the cost exceeding all expectations.

In order to give the prospective boatbuilder some idea of what the final cost will be on a selected project, the information in the paragraphs to follow have been provided. The prices, of course, will probably change slightly by the time you read this, but they should still be close enough to give you a ball park figure. If you want to come a little closer, compare the prices of one or two items in this book with current prices and then adjust the remaining items accordingly. For example, if the price of one item in this book is now listed at, say, $10, and upon checking the current price you find it to be $12, divide the former price into the latest price to obtain a correction factor for the other materials. That is, $12/$10 = 1.20; therefore, multiply all prices in this book by 1.2 to obtain an approximate current price.

The lumber price list in Figs. A-1A and A-1B was provided by Maurice L. Condon Co., of White Plains, New York, 10603, and represents a large array of boat lumber—complete enough to meet any amateur's or professional's needs. The prices should help you guesstimate the cost of the required lumber for your boat.

## FIBERGLASS MATERIALS

The following prices and descriptive data on fiberglass were obtained from Herter's, Inc. It should be sufficient to estimate the cost of either covering your entire boat or making minor repairs with such materials.

*Patching Kit No. 1:* Kit consisting of 1 pint of resin with hardening agent, 3 sq. ft. of fiberglass cloth, 6 linear feet of 2″ fiberglass tape, instructional manual, 1/4 pint resin or solvent...$5.66

## FIBERGLASS BOAT COVERING KITS

| Boat Size | Type |
|---|---|
| 10 ft. | Pram |
| 10 ft. | Pram |
| 12 ft. | Fishing or Outboard |
| 12 ft. | Fishing or Outboard |
| 14 ft. | Fishing or Outboard |
| 14 ft. | Fishing or Outboard |
| 16 ft. | Fishing or Outboard |
| 16 ft. | Fishing or Outboard |
| 12 ft. | Both ends pointed hunting boat |
| 12 ft. | Both ends pointed hunting boat |
| 15 ft. | Canoe |
| 17 ft. | Canoe |
| 18 ft. | Canoe |

| Area to Cover | Width of Cloth | Amount of cloth | Complete cost |
|---|---|---|---|
| Bottom only | 44″ | 3 1/2 yds. | $20.88 |
| Bottom, sides, transom | 38″ | 8 yds. | 39.89 |
| Bottom to splash rails | 60″ | 4 yds. | 29.29 |
| Bottom, sides, transom | 44″ | 9 yds. | 44.11 |
| Bottom to splash rails | 60″ | 5 yds. | 36.09 |
| Bottom, sides, transom | 44″ | 10 1/2 yds. | 54.78 |
| Bottom to splash rails | 60″ | 5 1/2 yds. | 41.32 |
| Bottom sides, transom | 50″ | 11 1/2 yds. | 61.00 |
| Bottom and sides only | 60″ | 4 yds. | 29.29 |
| Bottom & sides & deck | 60″ | 5 yds. | 36.05 |
| Replace all canvas with Fiberglass cloth | 60″ | 5 yds. | 36.05 |
| Replace all canvas with Fiberglass cloth | 60″ | 6 yds. | 42.88 |
| Replace all canvas with Fiberglass cloth | 60″ | 6 1/3 yds. | 47.59 |

Prices for other accessories, parts, etc., may be obtained from the manufacturers listed in Chapter 3. However, the major items in a boat hull will be the lumber, and perhaps the fiberglass coating—the fastenings will normally be a minor part of the total cost.

Tel: 914-946-4111      MAURICE L. CONDON CO., INC.            September 1976
                          250 Ferris Avenue
                       White Plains, New York 10603

MILLWORK: Planing and ripping only.  Special millwork prices on request.
NOTE: Lumber in stock already D2S, add 10¢ BF.TEAK already D2S, add 15¢
MINIMUM MILL CHARGE-small orders-Planing $3.00  Ripping $3.00
SELECTED OR CUT STOCK-add 25% QUANTITY PRICES ON REQUEST
YARD HOURS: Mon. thru Fri. 8AM to 4:30PM (No yard service between 12:00-1PM)
SATURDAYS-8AM to 2PM (Closed Saturdays during June, July, & August)
ALL PRICES F.O.B. OUR YARD & SUBJECT TO CHANGE WITHOUT NOTICE

| | 1000 BF | Under 1000 BF | UNDER 100 BF |
| --- | --- | --- | --- |
| SITKA SPRUCE B & BETTER VG ROUGH | | | |
| 1 x 4 Special Selected Grain x RL | $1.29 | $1.44 | $1.64 |
| 1" 1¼" 1½" 2" thickness | | | |
|   6"-7" wide x 8'-15' | $1.15 | $1.30 | $1.50 |
|   6"-7" wide x16'-20' | $1.45 | $1.60 | $1.80 |
|   6"-7" wide x21'-24' | $1.75 | $1.90 | $2.10 |
|   6"-7" wide x25'-29' | $1.95 | $2.10 | $2.30 |
|   6"-7" wide x30' up | $2.15 | $2.30 | $2.50 |
| Widths 8" and wider - ADD 15¢ BF | | | |
| 3x3 and 4x4 x RL | $1.45 | $1.60 | $1.90 |
| 3" & thicker x 6" up x 16'-26' | $1.80 | $1.90 | $2.10 |
| 3" & thicker x 6" up x 27' up | $1.90 | $2.00 | $2.20 |
| SELECTED FOR AIRCRAFT - ADD 10¢ BF | | | |
| PHILIPPINE MAHOGANY DARK RED FAS GRADE ROUGH, 6"-11" wide, 8' to 15' long | | | |
| 1" thickness | 82¢ BF | 92¢ BF | $1.02 BF |
| 1¼" " | 83¢ BF | 93¢ BF | $1.03 BF |
| 1½" " | 84¢ BF | 94¢ BF | $1.04 BF |
| 2" " | 86¢ BF | 96¢ BF | $1.06 BF |

Widths 12"-17" wide, add 15¢ BF    Lengths 16' up, add 10¢ BF
Widths 18" and up, add 30¢ BF
3" and 4" thickness, prices on request

| | | | |
|---|---|---|---|
| AFRICAN MAHOGANY FAS GRADE ROUGH, 6" to 11" wide, 8' to 15' long | | | |
| 1" thickness | 80¢ BF | 90¢ BF | $1.10 BF |
| 1¼" " | 81¢ BF | 91¢ BF | $1.11 BF |
| 1½" " | 82¢ BF | 92¢ BF | $1.12 BF |
| 2" " | 85¢ BF | 95¢ BF | $1.15 BF |
| Widths 12"-14" wide, add 10¢ BF, Stock 15" and wider on request | | | |
| Lengths 16'-19' add 10¢ BF, 20'-22' add 15¢ BF, 23' up add 20¢ BF | | | |
| 3" and 4" thickness, prices on request | | | |
| HONDURAS MAHOGANY FAS GRADE ROUGH, 6" to 11" wide, 8'-15' long | | | |
| 1" thickness | $1.10 BF | $1.20 BF | $1.30 BF |
| 1¼" " | $1.11 BF | $1.21 BF | $1.31 BF |
| 1½" " | $1.12 BF | $1.22 BF | $1.32 BF |
| 2" " | $1.15 BF | $1.25 BF | $1.35 BF |
| Widths 12"-14" wide, add 10¢ BF, Stock 15" and wider on request | | | |
| Lengths 16'-19' add 10¢ BF, 20'-22' add 15¢ BF, 23'up add 20¢ BF | | | |
| 3" and 4" thickness, prices on request | | | |
| TEAK FAS GRADE ROUGH, 6"-11" wide, 6'-15' long | | | |
| 1" thickness | $2.80 BF | $2.90 BF | $3.05 BF |
| 1¼" " | $2.85 BF | $2.95 BF | $3.10 BF |
| 1½" " | $2.90 BF | $3.00 BF | $3.15 BF |
| 2" " | $3.00 BF | $3.10 BF | $3.25 BF |
| 3" " | $3.50 BF | $3.50 BF | $3.50 BF |
| 4" " | $3.60 BF | $3.60 BF | $3.60 BF |
| 6" " | $3.70 BF | $3.70 BF | $3.70 BF |
| Widths: 12"-14" wide, add 40¢ BF, 15" up, add 60¢ BF | | | |
| Lengths: 16'-20', add 20¢ BF, 21' up, add 40¢ BF | | | |

Fig. A-1. Boatbuilding costs.

CLEAR DOUGLAS FIR, VG AND FG, Dry, Rough.

| | | | |
|---|---|---|---|
| 1" thickness, 1¼" & 2" | $1.18 BF | $1.28 BF | $1.43 BF |
| 3"       " | $1.20 BF | $1.30 BF | $1.45 BF |
| 4"       " | $1.30 BF | $1.40 BF | $1.55 BF |

Lengths 20' & over, add 20¢ BF
SPECIAL OFFER: 3" Flat Grain, Clear, 8"-10" wide x 14-16' $1.00 BF
NOTE-MINIMUM ORDER 100 BF

MIXED OAK FAS GRADE ROUGH, 6"-11" wide, 6' to 15' long

| | | | |
|---|---|---|---|
| 1" thickness | 80¢ BF | 80¢ BF | 90¢ BF |
| 1¼"       " | 82¢ BF | 82¢ BF | 92¢ BF |
| 1½"       " | 85¢ BF | 85¢ BF | 95¢ BF |
| 2"       " | 92¢ BF | 92¢ BF | $1.02 BF |

Widths 12" up add 10¢ BF lengths 16' add 10¢ BF - LONGER LENGTHS ON REQUEST
ALL WHITE OAK ROUGH, Add 10¢ BF to above prices.
3" and 4" thickness, prices on request

WESTERN RED CEDAR

| | | | |
|---|---|---|---|
| 1" D2S 3/4" x RW x RL | 84¢ BF | 95¢ BF | $1.05 BF |
| 2" D2S 1-3/4"    " | $1.07 BF | $1.17 BF | $1.27 BF |

VIRGINIA WHITE CEDAR FLITCH SAWN ROUGH

| | | | |
|---|---|---|---|
| 1" thickness | 72¢ BF | 82¢ BF | 92¢ BF |
| 1¼"       " | 77¢ BF | 87¢ BF | 97¢ BF |
| 2"       " | 82¢ BF | 92¢ BF | $1.02 BF |

ALASKAN YELLOW CEDAR ROUGH

| | | | |
|---|---|---|---|
| 1" thickness | 83¢ BF | 93¢ BF | $1.03 BF |
| 1¼"       " | 93¢ BF | $1.03 BF | $1.13 BF |

MAURICE L. CONDON CO., INC.　　　　September 1976
250 Ferris Avenue
White Plains, New York 10603

| | MARINE PLYWOOD | | | | | | |
|---|---|---|---|---|---|---|---|
| | 4x8 | 4x10 | 4x12 | 4x14 | 4x16 | 4x18 | 4x20 |
| FIR PLYWOOD (per SF) | | | | | | | |
| 1/4" | 58¢ | 65¢ | 67¢ | --- | 70¢ | --- | --- |
| 3/8" | 72¢ | 77¢ | 87¢ | --- | 87¢ | 90¢ | 90¢ |
| 1/2" | 83¢ | --- | 89¢ | --- | 1.01 | --- | --- |
| 5/8" | 94¢ | --- | --- | --- | --- | --- | --- |
| 3/4" | 1.08 | --- | 1.27 | --- | 1.27 | --- | --- |
| 1" | 1.30 | --- | --- | --- | --- | --- | --- |

SPECIAL ITEM  3/4" x 5' x 10' .......... $1.40 SF
BRUYNZEEL REGINA (Utile) MAHOGANY - Rotary Cut

| | 4x8 | 4x10 | 4x12 | 4x14 | 4x16 | 4x18 | 4x20 |
|---|---|---|---|---|---|---|---|
| 5/32 4MM | 71¢ | --- | 88¢ | --- | --- | --- | --- |
| 3/16 5MM | 81¢ | --- | --- | --- | --- | --- | --- |
| 1/4 6MM | 93¢ | 1.12 | 1.12 | --- | 1.12 | --- | --- |
| 5/16 8MM | 1.11 | --- | --- | --- | --- | --- | --- |
| 3/8 9MM | 1.21 | --- | 1.47 | --- | 1.60 | --- | --- |
| 1/2 12MM | 1.59 | --- | 1.84 | --- | 1.84 | --- | --- |
| 5/8 15MM | 1.82 | --- | 2.11 | --- | --- | --- | --- |
| 3/4 18MM | 2.21 | --- | 2.57 | --- | 2.57 | --- | --- |
| 1" 25MM | 3.00 | --- | --- | --- | --- | --- | --- |
| OCCUME MAHOGANY | | | | | | | |
| 1/8 3MM | 65¢ | --- | --- | --- | --- | --- | --- |
| 1/4 6MM | 80¢ | --- | 90¢ | --- | 90¢ | --- | --- |

Fig. A-1. Boatbuilding costs.

## PHILIPPINE MAHOGANY

| | Ribbon 2 Sides | | Ribbon/Rotary | | Rotary 2 Sides |
|---|---|---|---|---|---|
| 1/4 x 4 x 8 | 84¢ | 1/4 x 4 x 8 | 65¢ | 1/4 x 4 x 8 | 50¢ |
| 3/8 x 4 x 8 | 98¢ | 3/8 x 4 x 8 | 85¢ | 3/8 x 4 x 8 | 75¢ |
| 1/2 x 4 x 8 | 1.05 | 1/2 x 4 x 8 | 95¢ | 1/2 x 4 x 8 | 90¢ |
| 5/8 x 4 x 8 | ---- | 5/8 x 4 x 8 | 1.00 | 5/8 x 4 x 8 | ---- |
| 3/4 x 4 x 8 | 1.25 | 3/4 x 4 x 8 | 1.13 | 3/4 x 4 x 8 | 1.10 |

## TEAK MARINE PLYWOOD

| | Teak One Face | Teak Two Faces |
|---|---|---|
| 11/64 x 4 x 8 | $1.85 SF | ---- |
| 1/4 x 4 x 8 | $2.02 SF | $2.79 SF |
| 3/8 x 4 x 8 | $2.26 SF | ---- |
| 1/2 x 4 x 8 | $2.52 SF | $2.91 SF |
| 5/8 x 4 x 8 | $2.71 SF | $3.23 SF |
| 3/4 x 4 x 8 | $3.16 SF | $3.43 SF |

## TEAK MARINE PLYDEK

1/4 x 4 x 8 Black Line at $2.40 SF    1/4 x 4 x 8 White Line $2.50 SF

SPECIAL OFFER                         SPECIAL OFFER
SAFARI (utile) MARINE PLYWOOD
4MM 5/32 x 4 x 8 @ 50¢ SF    6MM  1/4 x 4 x 8  @ 70¢ SF

## AIRCRAFT GRADE PLYWOOD (Poplar Core)
### Mil. Spec. P 6070   90 Degree Angle

| AFRICAN MAHOGANY | | BIRCH | |
|---|---|---|---|
| 1/16 x 4 x 8 | @ $1.28SF | 1/16 x 4 x 4 | @ $ .80 SF |
| 3/32 x 4 x 8 | @ $1.16SF | 1/16 x 4 x 8 | @ $1.35 SF |
| 1/8 x 4 x 8 | @ $1.20SF | 3/32 x 4 x 8 | @ $1.04 SF |
| 3/16 x 4 x 8 | @ $1.28SF | 1/8 x 4 x 8 | @ $1.07 SF |
| 1/4 x 4 x 8 | @ $1.44SF | 3/16x 4 x 8 | @ $1.26 SF |
| | | 1/4 x 4 x 8 | @ $1.50 SF |

```
PLYWOOD BUNDLING CHARGES (per bundle)
Size  4 x 8      $6.00 flat charge
Size  4 x10-12  $8.00        "
Size  4 x14-16  $10.00       "
Size  4x18'20   $12.50       "

PHILIPPINE MAHOGANY MOULDING
1/4" Quarter-Round        35¢ LF
1/2"      "               35¢ LF
3/4"      "               35¢ LF
3/4" Half-Round           35¢ LF
1"   Half-Round           45¢ LF
1-1/4"    "               45¢ LF
1-1/2"    "               45¢ LF

DECK PLUGS  (price per 100)
              3/8"     1/2"     5/8"
Mahogany    $2.40    $2.60    $2.90
Teak        $2.90    $3.60    $4.25

GLUE -     WELDWOOD WATER RESISTANT
           5 lbs.  $7.00 each
           1 lb.   $2.10 each
           8 Oz.   $1.40 each

         WELDWOOD RESORCINOL WATERPROOF
           1 Gallon $30.00 each
           1 Quart  $ 9.50 each
           1 Pint   $ 6.50 each
           1/4 Pint $ 2.25 each

NOTE: If shipped, plus postage & handling
```

Fig. A-1. Boatbuilding costs.

## KNOTS FOR BOATMEN

Every "Old Salt" knows his knots, and the amateur boatbuilder—once his craft is launched—will find that he should know a few himself—for tying mooring loops, splicing broken rigging ropes—the cases are endless.

End knots, for example, have the double purpose of preventing the strands from fraying and also serve as a "stopper" to prevent the rope end from pulling through a loop or sheave. While there are several ways of tying end knots, the end or back splice is the neatest permanent-end knot. Figure A-2 (A through E) shows how this knot is tied. One trick in finishing any splice like this is to separate the yarns when the knot is at the half completed stage and slip away approximately half the fibers of each. When the finishing tucks are made, the knot will tape neatly into the standing part.

The eye splice (Fig. A-3) can be used to form a fixed loop of almost any desired size. It will not jam under strain and for this reason can be easily untied. Although the primary purpose of the eye splice is to form a fixed loop or eye in the end of a rope—like for a mooring loop—the same splice can be used to splice one rope into the side of another rope to form a lateral. To make this splice, unwind the strands at the end of the rope four to six turns and bend the end back on the standing part to such a distance as will form a loop or eye of the desired size. Then proceed to tuck the strands one over and one under. After two or three tucks (Fig. A-3) trim the strands as previously described and finish tucking until the strands are taken up; then trim the ends flush with the windings, or lay of the rope.

The sheet bend (Fig. A-4) and the square knot (Fig. A-5) are practical for joining ends of rope or cord of all common sizes, or if you prefer a neater-looking splice try the short rope splice shown in Fig. A-6. The long splice (Fig. A-7) may also be used. Here the strands of both ends are unlaid for a distance equal to six or seven times the circumference of the rope. Then the ends are placed together with strands 1 and 2 and A and B in position as shown in the figure. Unlay strand 1 along the standing part and replace with strand 1. Unlay and replace the corresponding strands in the opposite direction along the standing part, leaving enough at each of the ends to make an overhand crossing—the latter being the same as the first crossing in the

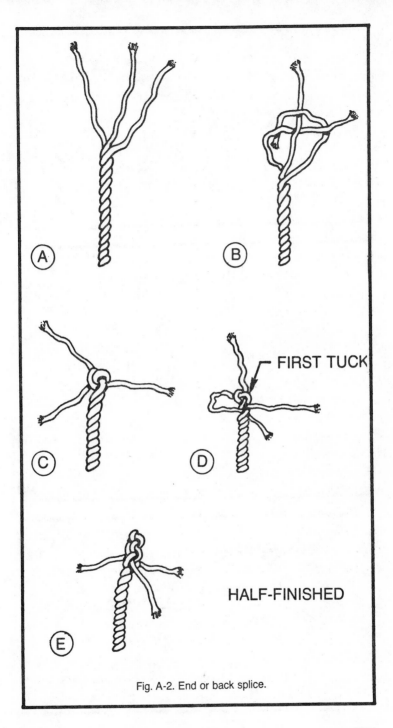

FIRST TUCK

HALF-FINISHED

Fig. A-2. End or back splice.

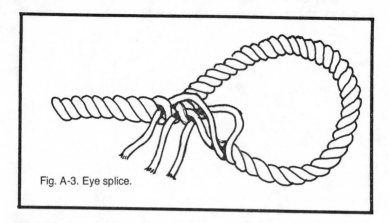

Fig. A-3. Eye splice.

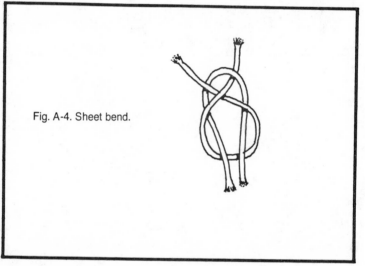

Fig. A-4. Sheet bend.

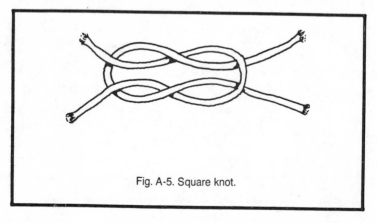

Fig. A-5. Square knot.

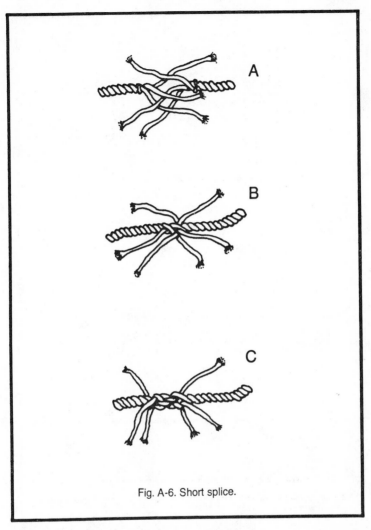

Fig. A-6. Short splice.

square knot. Strands A and B at the center and those at the ends then are joined with overhand crossings and the free ends of the strands at the ends of the splice are tucked over and under once as done in the short splice (Fig. A-6). Do the same with strands A and B at the center. Trim away about half of each strand and make at least two more tucks. Then pound the tucks and crossings into the lay of the rope and cut the ends of the strands flush with the lay. It is essential to keep the strands of this splice—and any other splice for that matter—pulled tight as successive tucks are made.

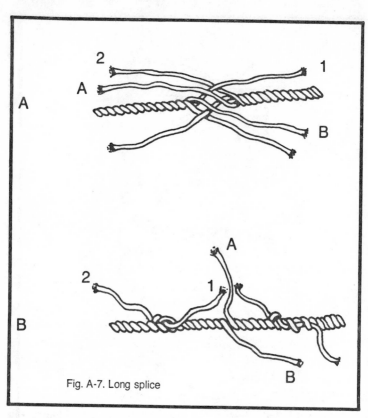

Fig. A-7. Long splice

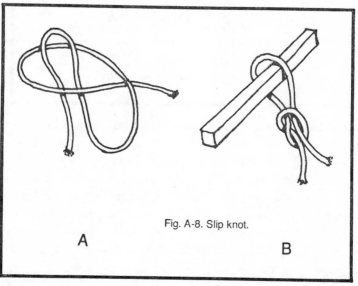

Fig. A-8. Slip knot.

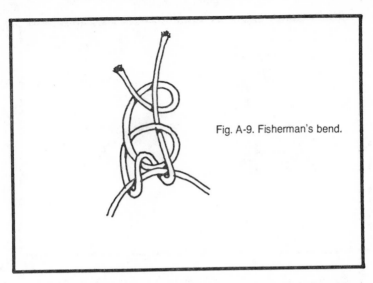

Fig. A-9. Fisherman's bend.

Where a slip knot is to be tied over a pole, bar, or similar object where the loop will pass over it easily, tie the knot with the standing part as shown in Fig. A-8A. This will prevent the knot from jamming under sudden strain. Where the object is closed at both ends the rope is carried around it and an overhand is tied on the standing part as shown in Fig. A-8B.

Figures A-9, A-10, and A-11 show various hitches which are commonly used to attach ropes to objects of different shapes and sizes. One of the simplest and most effective of these is the clove

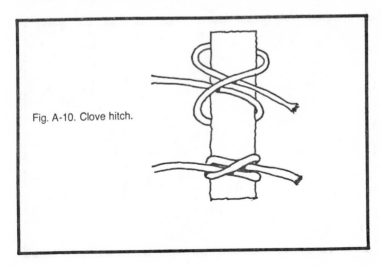

Fig. A-10. Clove hitch.

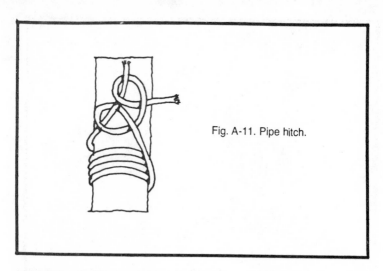

Fig. A-11. Pipe hitch.

hitch (Fig. A-10) since the rope passes around the object in one direction—causing no twisting strain on the strands.

One of the quickest ways of tying a fixed loop in a rope is by use of the bowline knot shown in Fig. A-12. Properly tied, the bowline knot will never slip, pull out, or jam under any strain the rope will hold. The knot is furthermore easy to untie due to the nature of the turns. The bowline begins with an overhand loop in the standing part, spaced to give a fixed loop of the desired size. Along the same line is the double bowline which makes the well-known "boatswain's chair." When used in rescue or other work, one loop serves as a

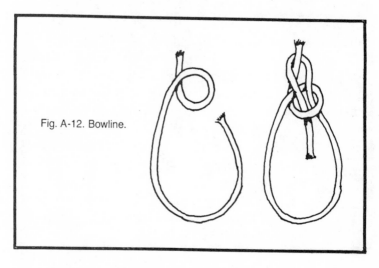

Fig. A-12. Bowline.

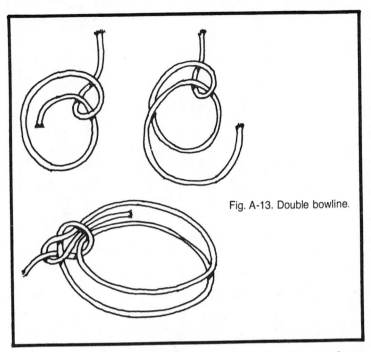

Fig. A-13. Double bowline.

"seat" while the other loop forms a back rest, leaving the arms free. Details of the double bowline are shown in Fig. A-13.

## WEATHER WISDOM

Any boater who is out on big water is essentially at the mercy of the weather. For this reason, every boater should have a basic knowledge of weather forecasting in order to take the necessary precautions to prevent any ill effects from the weather.

In most cases, when the weather is about to change, it will send signs in advance, and the alert amateur should be responsive to them. The weather's three ways of announcing a break are a change in air pressure, a change in wind direction, and a change in cloud formation. The professional forecaster will have various instruments designed to observe and record these changes, but for the amateur boater—in a small specific area—your own observations are likely to be more reliable.

The table in Fig. A-14 is intended to be used as a guide to show roughly what may be expected—weather-wise—from various observations on both land and sea.

| BEAUFORT NUMBER | DESCRIPTIVE TERM | VELOCITY EQUIVALENT AT A STANDARD HEIGHT OF 10 METRES ABOVE OPEN FLAT GROUND | | | | | Land |
| --- | --- | --- | --- | --- | --- | --- | --- |
| | | mean velocity in knots | metres/sec | km/h | m.p.h. | | |
| 0 | Calm | <1 | 0 – 0·2 | <1 | <1 | | Calm; smoke rises vertically |
| 1 | Light air | 1 – 3 | 0·3 – 1·5 | 1 – 5 | 1 – 3 | | Direction of wind shown by smoke drift but not by windvanes |
| 2 | Light breeze | 4 – 6 | 1·6 – 3·3 | 6 – 11 | 4 – 7 | | Wind felt on face; leaves rustle; ordinary vanes moved by wind |
| 3 | Gentle breeze | 7 – 10 | 3·4 – 5·4 | 12 – 19 | 8 – 12 | | Leaves and small twigs in constant motion; wind extends light flag |
| 4 | Moderate breeze | 11 – 16 | 5·5 – 7·9 | 20 – 28 | 13 – 18 | | Raises dust and loose paper; small branches are moved |
| 5 | Fresh breeze | 17 – 21 | 8·0 – 10·7 | 29 – 38 | 19 – 24 | | Small trees in leaf begin to sway; crested wavelets form on inland waters |
| 6 | Strong breeze | 22 – 27 | 10·8 – 13·8 | 39 – 49 | 25 – 31 | | Large branches in motion; whistling heard in telegraph wires; umbrellas used with difficulty |
| 7 | Near gale | 28 – 33 | 13·9 – 17·1 | 50 – 61 | 32 – 38 | | Whole trees in motion; inconvenience felt when walking against wind |
| 8 | Gale | 34 – 40 | 17·2 – 20·7 | 62 – 74 | 39 – 46 | | Breaks twigs off trees; generally impedes progress |

Table A-1. Velocity Equivalent At A Standard Height Of 10 Meters Above Open Flat Ground.

| No. | Description | | | | | Effects |
|---|---|---|---|---|---|---|
| 9 | Strong gale | 41 – 47 | 20·8 – 24·4 | 75 – 88 | 47 – 54 | Slight structural damage occurs (chimney pots and slates removed) |
| 10 | Storm | 48 – 55 | 24·5 – 28·4 | 89 – 102 | 55 – 63 | Seldom experienced inland; trees uprooted; considerable structural damage occurs |
| 11 | Violent storm | 56 – 63 | 28·5 – 32·6 | 103 – 117 | 64 – 72 | Very rarely experienced; accompanied by widespread damage |
| 12 | Hurricane. | 64 – 71 | 32·7 – 36·9 | 118 – 133 | 73 – 82 | — |
| 13 | — | 72 – 80 | 37·0 – 41·4 | 134 – 149 | 83 – 92 | — |
| 14 | — | 81 – 89 | 41·5 – 46·1 | 150 – 166 | 93 – 103 | — |
| 15 | — | 90 – 99 | 46·2 – 50·9 | 167 – 183 | 104 – 114 | — |
| 16 | — | 100 – 108 | 51·0 – 56·0 | 184 – 201 | 115 – 125 | — |
| 17 | — | 109 – 118 | 56·1 – 61·2 | 202 – 220 | 126 – 136 | — |

Table A-2. Wave Heights.

| SPECIFICATIONS | | Probable wave height* in metres | Probable wave height* in feet |
|---|---|---|---|
| Sea | Coast | | |
| Sea like a mirror | Calm | — | — |
| Ripples with the appearance of scales are formed, but without foam crests | Fishing smack just has steerage way | 0·1 (0·1) | ¼ (¼) |
| Small wavelets; still short but more pronounced; crests have a glassy appearance and do not break | Wind fills the sails of smacks which then travel at about 1-2 miles per hour | 0·2 (0·3) | ½ (1) |
| Large wavelets; crests begin to break; foam of glassy appearance; perhaps scattered white horses | Smacks begin to careen and travel about 3-4 miles per hour | 0·6 (1) | 2 (3) |
| Small waves, becoming longer; fairly frequent white horses | Good working breeze, smacks carry all canvas with good list | 1 (1·5) | 3½ (5) |
| Moderate waves, taking a more pronounced long form; many white horses are formed (chance of some spray) | Smacks shorten sail | 2 (2·5) | 6 (8½) |
| Large waves begin to form; the white foam crests are more extensive everywhere (probably some spray) | Smacks have double reef in mainsail; care required when fishing | 3 (4) | 9½ (13) |
| Sea heaps up and white foam from breaking waves begins to be blown in streaks along the direction of the wind | Smacks remain in harbour and those at sea lie-to | 4 (5·5) | 13½ (19) |
| Moderately high waves of greater length; edges of crests begin to break into the spindrift; the foam is blown in well-marked streaks along the direction of the wind | All smacks make for harbour, if near | 5·5 (7·5) | 18 (25) |

| | | | |
|---|---|---|---|
| 7 (10) | 23 (32) | — | High waves; dense streaks of foam along the direction of the wind; crests of waves begin to topple, tumble and roll over; spray may affect visibility |
| 9 (12·5) | 29 (41) | — | Very high waves with long overhanging crests; the resulting foam, in great patches, is blown in dense white streaks along the direction of the wind; on the whole, the surface of the sea takes a white appearance; the tumbling of the sea becomes heavy and shock-like; visibility affected |
| 11·5 (16) | 37 (52) | — | Exceptionally high waves (small and medium-sized ships might be for a time lost to view behind the waves); the sea is completely covered with long white patches of foam lying along the direction of the wind; everywhere the edges of the wave crests are blown into froth; visibility affected |
| 14 (—) | 45 (—) | — | The air is filled with foam and spray; sea completely white with driving spray; visibility very seriously affected |
| — | — | — | |
| — | — | — | |
| — | — | — | |
| — | — | — | |
| — | — | — | |

# Index